The FILMS of
WORLD WAR II

The FILMS of WORLD WAR II

by JOE MORELLA, EDWARD Z. EPSTEIN, and JOHN GRIGGS

Introduction by Judith Crist

The Citadel Press   Secaucus, New Jersey

To our families
and to all those who made
the films of World War II

Special thanks to Dore Schary, Leonard Spigelgass,
Allen Rivkin, Bob Smith, Ilene Wagner, Patrick Bryan,
Patrick B. Clark, David C. L'Heureux, John Madden,
Lou Valentino, Jack Haber and the USO; and very
special thanks to Judith Crist.

First paperbound printing, 1975
Copyright © 1973 by Joe Morella, Edward Z. Epstein & John Griggs
All rights reserved
Published by Citadel Press
A division of Lyle Stuart, Inc.
120 Enterprise Ave., Secaucus, N.J. 07094
In Canada: George J. McLeod Limited
73 Bathurst St., Toronto, Ont.
Manufactured in the United States of America by
Halliday Lithograph Corp., West Hanover, Mass.
Designed by William Meinhardt

ISBN 0-8065-0482-X

Introduction
by JUDITH CRIST

We were war-lovers in my movie-going generation and lovers of war movies, the movies of World War II, we have remained, joined by other generations for the very best of some very obvious and some rather subtle reasons.

We were war-lovers in an age of innocence, and certainly it is difficult to explain to new generations, as firm as we were in their conviction that the entire world was born yesterday, just how romantic the Depression children of the thirties could be. The romanticism flourished in our isolation, largely a matter of economics within the United States in that pre-air age, and a matter of politics in relation to the world. We were the disillusioned who were learning that the world had not been made safe for democracy; we learned our lessons from *All Quiet on the Western Front* and from the gritty poverty films that filled the breadlines with embittered veterans. We went on peace strikes (how quaint our chant of "No more battleships—we want schools"!) and the boys at Harvard formed The Veterans of Future Wars, between swallows of goldfish. There were monsters of evil abroad: a bright revue lampooned Hitler, Mussolini and Hirohito (Stalin, of course, was still in the good-guy category) as "angels of peace" who were grab-bing pieces of Europe and Africa and Asia—but *Grand Hotel, Cavalcade, It Happened One Night, Mutiny on the Bounty, The Great Ziegfeld, The Life of Emile Zola, You Can't Take It With You, Gone with the Wind* and *Rebecca* were the Oscar-winning films that beguiled us during the thirties, all roman-tic in their view of time past or cheerful in the rare glimpse of the present, and all but the monumental *GWTW* in physical and moral tones of black and white.

And therein was the innocence—and the romanti-cism. Only the very wise, and even they needed the insight of historic perspective, had inklings of the complexities of the Spanish Civil War, which brought battle to "our" kind of civilization on the Continent. Certainly no adolescent saw it as a cynical arms-test-ing ground for red and black dictatorships. The "thinking" adolescent had gone beyond the school-boy and the butterfly of *All Quiet;* the master war-lover of that generation had put the machismo mark on warfare with *A Farewell to Arms* (and if Helen Hayes died and left Gary Cooper to his ambulance-driving, it was a matter of morals rather than mor-tality and the mechanics of *Love Story* are eternal), so that in our deepest hearts we yearned for a dedication and a testing ground—and how we envied and admired the older boys who could join the Abraham Lincoln Brigade and find the earth moving via sleeping bags and beautiful loyalists. (By the time Hollywood got around to *For Whom the Bell Tolls* it had been quite thoroughly bowdlerized, morally and politically, with James Agee's memorable comment at the time that the word "nationalist" had been substituted for the "fascist" of Dudley Nichols' script and "I thought I once heard the word Falangist, but it may have been fuh land sakes.")

The romanticism crashed up against the political realities of the late thirties, made clear even to adolescents by international correspondents in print and by radio, in newsreels and in the trickle of refugees from the flickering holocaust. The tragedies abroad brought twists and turns at home, with strange fellows sharing beds when pacifist socialists found themselves with the isolationist America First and the internationalists saw the Moscow-manipulated League Against War and Fascism become the League for Peace and Democracy during the Nazi-Soviet pact. But then in no time the schoolgirls knitting for Bundles for Britain were extending their needles to Russian War Relief. And we bought our share of *The Grand Illusion*.

For those of us with an awareness, Hollywood's early acknowledgments of the state of the world were comforting; in their simplistics, their naivetes, they insulted the intelligence, but intelligence was rarely a factor in one's acceptance of Shadowland. We knew the good guys and the bad guys and it was for this definition that we looked and in whose reflection we found comfort. It was the humanism of the good guys versus the ruthless disregard of individuals displayed by the bad guys that counted; in the Hitchcock metaphor, the good guys worried about little old ladies or fragile diplomats who disappeared, while the villains, in or out of uniform, worked for the destruction of all for the power principle. And perhaps as never before we needed reassurance that the good guys could win. For anyone with the least information, Hitler was hardly the ridiculous clown of *The Great Dictator;* indeed Chaplin himself has said that had he known of the mass slaughter of the Jews he would not have made the film. But what counted most, perhaps, was that the film was made at all at a time when many still thought Hitler could be pacified, if not quite laughed out of existence; at very least the film articulated a hope that—well, that there was hope.

Thus, with few exceptions, the films of World War II were to be taken, in contemporary terms, with a grain of salted popcorn. The run of the Hollywood factory mill was aimed at the middle of the brow and the twelve-year-old mentality that Hollywood served until the mid-fifties, when television took away that vulnerable audience. And twelve-year-olds must be treated gently, spared the actualities, reassured, bolstered in an infantile conviction that the pure in heart (who else but us?) would triumph against all odds (who else but nasty Nazis and then the nasty Nips who, as a popular song declared, would soon be brought low on their "Japan-knees"?). Thus, before we were involved, we could enjoy Tyrone Power swaggering off to give the RAF a hand (only so that he could inherit a fortune), find the British quaint, and, albeit after having to perform heroics at Dunkirk to prove his seriousness, walk off into the sun with Betty Grable firmly his, even though her other arm is linked through that of his British rival. Not for us the careful detail and structure of *In Which We Serve:* that brave handful (how else conjure up the heritage of Valley Forge?) had to make a stand against the multitudes on Bataan, at Guadalcanal, on the Sahara, much the way the white-hatted minority had stood against black-hatted villainy in the Old West. The horses yielded to tanks—but it was still a range war.

The Russians, the Norwegians, the Free French (was there indeed a Frenchman loyal to Vichy, the way Hollywood hacks saw it?) all became perfection; the kid from Brooklyn, from Iowa, the Texas Division composed of Dakotans and Tennesseeans and Minnesotans, fought and died antiseptically after mouthing suitable clichés. And it was good and it was simple-minded and it was purgative, giving us relief from all the grimmer truths of the headlines, all the complications of survival and all the complexities of ongoing life. The plasticity of the people in that preplastic era is overwhelming to look at today—and even then they had a celluloid crackle that was a pleasant unreality, a slick-story step away from the embittered letters from the front, from the death lists, from the profiteering and the politicking. Andy Hardy didn't go to war—but he and his folks got a special Oscar in 1942 for "furthering the American way of life."

Midway in our involvement in the war a reality began to creep in, with real footage of air battles, of naval encounters and of infantry attacks spliced in. True accounts and diaries of men who knew war emerged and on rare occasions the feel and the grit of experience penetrated a film, for the most part in movies that came as the war ended. Fine documents— *San Pietro, The Battle of Britain*—were to be released later. But for the duration the security blanket of illusion kept us warm: every boy a potential hero, every mom a bundle of cheer, every girl a patient page-boyed Penelope.

It is strange, in retrospect, to consider how a nation, united as never before (and possibly since) by the attack on Pearl Harbor, sought simplifications. Actually, we wanted it that way—or perhaps we needed it. The issues were clear-cut; we wanted no tonings. And we got none. And only a cynic would note that Hollywood went all the way because the alternative was government control, and what the hell, the German and Italian and Japanese markets were gone, so why not make the nasties as nasty as the public stomach (and production code) would allow? Nobility was for our side, whether it was the brave G.I., the sacrificial partisan, the delectable Mrs. Miniver, or Claudette Colbert, in a never-never $2,400,000 Selznick soap opera world of chic mom working in a factory, a loyal mammy messin' 'round the house after her own factory shift was over, two cutesy-poo daughters, Monty Woolley as a refugee boarder all comically Anglo-Saxon, and a loyal bachelor beau on hand to step right in if dad really turned out to be missing in action.

Which of these fantasies can endure? *Casablanca* is certainly the most durable, enchanting today's young as it did us, because it is the dreamland epitomized in Rick's café, with the rootless American the nobleman, the quaint refugees the sweet souls, the exquisite woman weakened briefly by passion settling for the *oblige* of *noblesse,* the nasty Nazi nasty to the end, but the civilized Frenchman decently corruptible and corruptibly decent at the fadeout. No need to ponder the vintage of Dooley Wilson's case of do or die; it's timeless schmaltz, with the Marseillaise to stir the blood, dialect comedians to make us internationally tolerant and Bogey to remind us that there will always be an Amurrican around who'll do the right thing—eventually. And for obvious reasons of romanticism and subtle reasons of security, young and old can cuddle up to its kitsch.

For my generation, the trashiest of the films of World War II are worth looking at, if only in their recall of a time of innocence, of a purity of morality that has vanished in the decades that saw the Japanese and German movie markets restored by films that showed the Americans as bumbling venal idiots and the Germans and Japanese as clear-headed strategists whose principles, but never their missles, may have been misguided—after all, they were deluded and/or enslaved. And the best of the films bear near-documentary testament, as *The Story of G.I. Joe* perhaps does best of all, to what the war was like for ordinary soldiers who, at best, saw a clearcut issue at stake or, at worst, a job assigned.

It was, of course, the last war that involved the passions of a people, and even that is a generalization we have learned did not hold true for many Americans. It was the first war that involved the film factories in an all-out propaganda battle—and certainly at this point, two wars later, the last. The Korean war produced cheapjack variations on the slant-eyed-Commies theme not too distant from the World War II films; the Vietnam war has produced no extensive fictions. Either we have reached the realization that war does not bear fictionalization and that the time is past for film to declare war good or bad, or television has taken over the audio-visual job of informing—and convincing.

In our present cinematic sophistication (and perhaps it involves our psychological and social growth as well), most of the films of World War II will tell us relatively little about that long-ago conflict. But they will tell us, largely by indirection, a great deal about the American people of the time—and therein is recorded history.

Contents

Foreword

The Films of World War II is the story of Hollywood's role in wartime, of the film industry's efforts toward victory and its contributions to the fight, of the effect of the war on Hollywood itself. It is the story, too, of the hard work done and the sacrifices made, sometimes heartbreaking, by the movie people themselves—a group frequently considered by the public at large as the most self-centered, self-indulgent collection of human beings in American society.

This is a telling of their work and their achievements, of their triumphs and failures, of good films and bad. Here are the stars who ascended during the war, here are those who waned. Here are Hollywood's heroes of the screen and heroes of the battlefields, and those who fought both the real and the imaginary battles.

Here they are . . . the G.I. Joes and the Doughgirls of Hollywood, from the sound stages to the bond drives to the Hollywood Canteen; from Sunset and Vine to Corregidor and Omaha Beach. In the air, on land, at sea—at home and abroad—Hollywood did its part. And this is the story of how it was done. . . .

Before the Battle

Even before the Japanese attacked Pearl Harbor there existed in Hollywood the Motion Picture Committee Cooperating for National Defense which had been formed to distribute and exhibit, without cost, national defense films produced by various government bureaus. After Pearl Harbor this group became the War Activities Committee, whose purpose was to coordinate the activities of the film industry with the national defense effort. Among the films that were circulated before Pearl Harbor were recruitment films seeking volunteers for the armed services and workers for defense-oriented industry. James Stewart appeared in *Winning Your Wings* and Clark Gable in *Wings Up,* and thousands who saw them volunteered for the air forces. Mrs. Roosevelt wrote and edited and Katharine Hepburn narrated *Women In Defense,* a film designed to encourage women either to join the armed forces or take jobs in defense plants.

In June 1942 the government established the Office of War Information as a single central contact with the film industry. Through this agency Hollywood and Washington worked together. Prints of all Hollywood features and shorts were made available, free of charge, to the Army overseas and to the Navy on ships everywhere. By the war's end over 43,000 prints of films had been shipped for viewing by American men in uniform. No other industry made its product available to the government without charge.

Almost everyone in Hollywood became involved in making training films for both industry and the armed forces. By 1944 the output of these films had reached a level of twenty per week and their value to the war effort was great. As producer Dore Schary remembers, "The film industry garnered praise from General Eisenhower, who during the war said that training films had cut the actual training period down to such an extent that our Army was better equipped to fight far sooner than they would have been without what was done by the film industry."

In addition to the training films a number of noncommercial, government-sponsored propaganda films were produced by the Signal Corps unit headed by director Frank Capra, who was commissioned a Colonel. The *Why We Fight* series was made to goad the public into accepting a relinquishment of isolationism. Capra was among the 132 members of the Screen Directors Guild who were in uniform. All told, over 437 Hollywood industry personnel were commissioned officers in the Signal Corps, among them: Major John Huston, Lieutenant-Colonel Anatole Litvak and Lieutenant-Colonel Darryl F. Zanuck.

Zanuck, who was head of production at 20th Century-Fox, became a topic of discussion in Congress because during the first nine months of his active duty in the Signal Corps he continued to receive his $5000 per week salary from his company. One is inclined to think that the arrangement should have been a private matter between Zanuck and the company, but the government was very much concerned about salaries and had at one point in 1943 suggested that a ceiling of $25,000 or $70,000 would be applied to annual wages in Hollywood. That proposal caused a great stir in the studios and perhaps generated more excitement there than Pearl Harbor itself. But questions of pay aside, Col. Zanuck was always itching for excitement regardless of personal danger, and while filming *At the Front,* a documentary about the North African campaign, he was frequently in the thick of battle.

In addition to the hundreds who joined the Signal Corps, there were many other industry personnel in uniforms. Of the 240,000 persons employed in the production, distribution and exhibition of motion pictures, over 40,000 served in the armed forces, including from Hollywood forty-eight executives and producers, 230 members of the Screen Writers Guild, forty cameramen (many who were engaged in combat photography), seventy-five electricians and sound technicians, 453 film technicians, eighty machinists and about 2000 musicians.

Industry personnel unable to don uniforms contributed their services in other ways, most notably through the United Services Organization Camp Shows and Treasury Department Bond Sale Drives.

The United Services Organization Inc., internationally known as the USO, was formed in 1941 to provide recreation and entertainment for the men in the armed forces. When the Camp Shows division was formed, hundreds of actors, singers, comedians and other professional performers signed up to entertain the troops.

The Camp Shows were organized into four circuits: the Victory Circuit, which included over 600 army posts and naval stations with first-class theaters for performances; the Blue Circuit, which included 1150 camps without theater facilities; the Hospital Circuit, which included the veterans' hospitals; and the Fox Hole Circuit, which was the overseas tour. Before the war was over, more than 2,000 performers had traveled overseas to entertain Allied forces.

Two of the most widely traveled—and most popular—stars were Paulette Goddard and Joe E. Brown.

Miss Goddard made history by being the first civilian woman to fly over the Himalaya Mountains, during her tour of Southeast Asia's backlands in the China-Burma-India Theater.

Mr. Brown, whose airman son Don was killed in a bomber crash, was perhaps the most widely traveled star, covering over 150,000 miles between March, 1942 and February, 1944, paying his own expenses all the way except when he flew by Army plane. He was the first star to tour Alaska, the Aleutian Islands, the Southwest Pacific combat waters and the China-Burma-India theater. In 1944, the National Father's Day Committee presented an award to Brown, proclaiming him "Father to All Men Overseas."

Joe E. Brown's enormous popularity was matched only by that of Bob Hope, who was widely held to be the most popular male star on USO circuits. Frances Langford, who frequently toured with Hope, was the most popular female entertainer, and Dinah Shore was the most popular singer with servicemen.

Among the overseas travelers were Al Jolson, Eddie Cantor, Adolphe Menjou, Fredric March, Jack Benny, Martha Raye, Carole Landis, Mitzi Mayfair, Kay Francis, Jane Froman, Marlene Dietrich, Deanna Durbin, Ann Shirley, Louise Albritton, Bing Crosby, George Raft, the Andrews Sisters, Fred Astaire, Joan Blondell, Humphrey Bogart, Eddie Bracken, Mary Brian, James Cagney, Jack Carson, Gary Cooper, Linda Darnell, Nelson Eddy, Errol Flynn, John Garfield, Billy Gilbert, Marsha Hunt, Betty Hutton, Boris Karloff, Stan Laurel, Anna Lee, Anna May Wong, Joel McCrea, Sheila Rogers, Jean Darling, Eddie Foy Jr., Irene Manning, Raymond Massey, Phil Silvers, Wallace Beery, Grace Moore, Mayo Methot, Ray Milland, Judith Anderson, Keenan Wynn, Spencer Tracy, Pat O'Brien, Martha O'Driscoll, Ann Sheridan, Randolph Scott, Charles Ruggles, Edward G. Robinson, Luise Rainer, Ray Bolger, Una Merkel, Keenan Wynn, William Gargan, Andy Arcari, Patti Thomas, Majorie Reynolds, Ingrid Bergman, Oliver Hardy, Ella Logan, Jane Pickens, and Ann Sheridan.

In the three years after Pearl Harbor, over 3500 performers made more than 35,000 personal appearances for an immeasurable accomplishment in morale boosting, all of it on a strictly volunteer basis, and sometimes at personal risk, with performers playing near enemy lines.

On a closer-to-home basis, the Hollywood Canteen was opened in October, 1942, with Bette Davis, as its president, constantly on hand to welcome the more than two million servicemen who passed through its doors. The Canteen had a roster of volunteer workers that numbered over 50,000 and included a glittering array of Hollywood notables. Every night a big band played as men in uniform danced with Hedy Lamarr, Betty Grable, Olivia de Havilland, Miss Davis, Marlene Dietrich, Joan Crawford, and dozens of other glamorous stars. The stars also performed, waited on tables and washed dishes, all without pay.

On the financial front, Hollywood's contribution could be measured in very real terms of billions of dollars raised in history's most gigantic war-financing effort as filmdom personalities worked to sell War Bonds. Stars toured the nation encouraging citizens to invest in defense. Thousands of War-Bond premieres were held, with distributors supplying films free of charge to theater owners who sold bonds for admission. In addition, theaters acted as collection centers for strategic materials which were in short supply and by the end of 1944 had collected over 162,000 tons of vitally needed metals and other scrap material.

Not only were money and material collected at theaters, but blood donations as well were encouraged and collected, sometimes as the price of admission. Stars often turned up to give blood themselves and encourage moviegoers to visit blood banks and "save a life." And thanks to millions of American donors, thousands of wounded men survived.

World War II brought many changes and challenges to Hollywood as it did to the nation at large. It brought problems—which are discussed elsewhere in this book—and, ironically, prosperity. After peaking in the mid-thirties, weekly movie attendance had declined in 1941 to fifty-five million per week, but in 1944 almost 100 million Americans—two-thirds of the population—attended movies each week, and the studios prospered as never before. Escapist fare was the general order of the day, but Hollywood was aware too of the need for films extolling the virtues of democracy and exposing the horrors and savagery of totalitarian regimes. America's motion picture industry rose to the task of tending the spirit of a nation during a perilous time in its history.

Here is how Hollywood went to war. . . .

Prewar Propaganda

Hollywood took up the fight against fascism long before the disaster at Pearl Harbor. The industry had its group of knowing people who were aware of the growing menace of fascism and the inevitability of American involvement in the war raging in Europe. There was, however, a vast isolationist sentiment in the country as a whole and the "let's not get involved" crowd was both highly vocal and powerful. Of the more than one thousand films produced by Hollywood in the three years between Munich and Pearl Harbor, only fifty were anti-Nazi in theme. The bulk of Hollywood's product was non-controversial, escapist fare.

In the years between Hitler's invasion of Poland and the attack on Pearl Harbor Hollywood became considerably more concerned with the world situation. Funds were raised for the U.S.O., Russian War Relief, Greek War Relief, United China Relief, Bundles for Britain. Joan Crawford donated her $112,000 fee for a film to the Red Cross. Cary Grant split $100,000 between British and American war charities.

In the late 1930's the market for American films overseas shrank as films with anti-fascist themes be-

gan to be produced by American studios. From a small and vociferous group of individuals, these anti-fascist films brought the charge that Hollywood was inciting the American people to war. This group accused Hollywood of being one-sided in its approach to the war in Europe. The extreme left in particular was very much opposed to American involvement in the war during the days of the Russian-German non-aggression pact, and many suggested that some sort of conspiracy against Russia was afoot. Of course they changed their tune when Hitler's armies turned on Russia.

In opposition to these groups were the film industry leaders who saw the need for American intervention. Twentieth Century-Fox chief Darryl F. Zanuck spoke frequently in favor of America's entering the war and supporting the British. He also defended the industry against the isolationists' attacks. "If you charge us with being anti-Nazi, you are right," he told a convention of American Legionnaires. "And if you accuse us of producing films in the interest of preparedness and national defense, again you are right."

In 1941 a Senate subcommittee, chaired by Senator D. Worth Clark, held hearings to investigate Hollywood's alleged "war-mongering." Wendell Willkie was hired to defend the industry, and soon had the isolationists on the defensive. Willkie told the Senators, "If you charge that the motion picture industry as a whole and its leading executives as individuals are opposed to the Nazi dictatorship in Germany, if this is the case, there need be no investigation. We abhor everything Hitler represents."

"The whole matter was thrown the hell out of court," producer Dore Schary recalls. But shortly before the raid on Pearl Harbor, Senator Clark said the Congressional hearings would be resumed. Needless to say, after December 7 those plans were dropped.

Following are some of the films that prepared Americans, at least psychologically, for the struggle.

The FILMS of
WORLD WAR II

Gilbert Roland, Dorothy Lamour, Karen Morley, and Anthony Quinn in *The Last Train from Madrid.*

The Last Train from Madrid

Paramount

New York release date, June 18, 1937

Produced by George M. Arthur; directed by James Hogan; screenplay by Louis Stevens and Robert Wyler, from a story by Paul Harvey Fox and Elsie Fox.

CAST: Dorothy Lamour, Lew Ayres, Gilbert Roland, Karen Morley, Lionel Atwill, Helen Mack, Robert Cummings, Olympe Bradna, Anthony Quinn, Lee Bowman.

The Last Train from Madrid was touted as the first motion picture to use the controversial Spanish Civil War as a background; nevertheless, its story avoided any controversy and neither took a political stand or made any propagandistic statement. It revolved around the old familiar "Grand Hotel" plot device of having a group of socially and emotionally diverse people caught up in a common desperate situation. In this instance they were all trying to get aboard the last train from besieged Madrid to the safety of Valencia.

Although criticized in many circles for using the Spanish conflict at all, *The Last Train from Madrid* was little more than a melodramatic mixture of suspense and romantic intrigue.

THE NEW YORK TIMES:

The Last Train from Madrid should not be accepted too literally or too seriously. True, it treats of the Spanish revolution, but merely as Hollywood has, in the past, regarded the melodramatic turmoils of Ruritania and Zenda. It is simply a topical and different background for a glib little fiction. . . . Its sympathies, neither Loyalist nor Rebel, are clearly on the side of the Ruritanians. The cast, taken from Paramount's second-string list, is best served by Anthony Quinn.

Frank Nugent

NEWSWEEK:

Diffusing its action among a dozen characters . . . Hollywood's first film with the Spanish revolution for a background neither takes sides in the conflict nor captures very much of its drama and horror. Karen Morley, Gilbert Roland, and Lew Ayres lend steadying support to several less experienced but promising newcomers in the cast.

19

Franchot Tone, Robert Young, and Robert Taylor as the "three comrades."

Three Comrades

MGM

New York release date, June 3, 1938

Produced by Joseph L. Mankiewicz; directed by Frank Borzage; screenplay by F. Scott Fitzgerald and Edward E. Paramore, adapted from the book by Erich Maria Remarque.

CAST: Robert Taylor, Margaret Sullavan, Franchot Tone, Robert Young, Guy Kibbee, Lionel Atwill, Henry Hull, Charley Grapewin, Monty Woolley.

MGM provided some of its best talent for this film adaptation of Erich Maria Remarque's novel about three young German soldiers who tried to find some

Margaret Sullavan with Franchot Tone, Robert Taylor, and Robert Young.

Franchot Tone, Margaret Sullavan, Robert Taylor, and Robert Young drinking with Lionel Atwill.

reason for living in post-World War I Germany. All of them are united in their tender love for the same girl, who is dying of tuberculosis. There are moments of levity and deeply moving ones as well as the shadow of the world's unrest and the girl's illness cast a pall over the joys of youth.

Margaret Sullavan played the dying girl; Robert Taylor, the "comrade" she loved the most; and Franchot Tone and Robert Young were his friends.

As written by F. Scott Fitzgerald and Edward E. Paramore, directed by Frank Borzage and produced by Joseph L. Mankiewicz, the movie remained true to the spirit of Remarque's book, and the foreboding Nazi undertones in the Germany it depicted were not appreciated by American Bundists.

NEW YORK HERALD TRIBUNE:

Margaret Sullavan could not announce her return to the screen in a more distinctive manner than she does as the brave, wistful, ethereal Patricia Hollmann of Remarque's *Three Comrades.* She is a perfect choice for the role and gives a truly great performance. . . . Frank Borzage has directed the film with a fine understanding of the delicate nuances, and Robert Taylor, Franchot Tone and Robert Young are splen-

did. . . . The soul of the author, which glowed warmly through every page, becomes a living fire in a memorable motion picture.

Robert W. Dana

TIME:

Like many another able writer, F. Scott Fitzgerald has gone to Hollywood. In this script, with Edward E. Paramore, he tried to adapt Erich Maria Remarque's novel into a corrosive arraignment of Nazi Germany. They wrote a scene in which a poor Jew proclaimed his love for Germany, another in which a rich Jew refrained from cheating three young gentiles, a scene in which famed books, including Remarque's, were burned by Nazis. Hays office censorship left none of these scenes in the finished picture. Much political content is removed by a camera shot of a blowing newspaper dated October 1920, still more by removal of all definite party labels. What is left is a love story, beautifully told and consummately acted, but so drenched in hopelessness and heavy with the aroma of death, of wasted youth in a world of foggy shapes and nameless menaces, that its beauty and strength are often clouded and betrayed.

Henry Fonda, Leo Carrillo in *Block-ade*, the first major film to deal with leftist-socialist sympathies.

Blockade

United Artists

New York release date, June 16, 1938

Produced by Walter Wanger; directed by William Dieterle; screenplay by John Howard Lawson.

CAST: Madeleine Carroll, Henry Fonda, Leo Carrillo, John Halliday, Vladimir Sokoloff, Robert Warwick, Reginald Denny, Peter Godfrey, Katherine de Mille, William Davidson, Fred Kohler, Carlos de Valdez, Nick Thompson, George Houston, Lupita Tovar, Rosina Galli.

Producer Walter Wanger's film was the first to deal seriously with the Spanish Civil War, although it named neither Loyalist nor Republican. It was a sincere anti-war film with Henry Fonda as a young peace-loving farmer who has to take up arms to defend his land. There was also a romantic intrigue with Madeleine Carroll and much of the film relied on tried-and-true spy melodrama for excitement. But, for its time, this was a courageous and controversial statement about democratic ideals and the threat posed against freedom by fascism, even though the fascists weren't directly identified.

Blockade created a furor among fascist-minded countries, where it was banned. Even in the United States it was picketed in many cities and was not a box office hit.

Producer Wanger was not deterred by pre-release threats of difficulty, asserting: "Not only do we [in

Henry Fonda and Madeleine Carroll.

Hollywood] meekly take intimidation from abroad, but we jump obediently when almost anybody in this country says 'Frog!' It's ridiculous, and I, for one, don't intend to continue. I'm going to release this Spanish picture as is, and if it's banned in Europe, I'll have to take my loss."

THE NEW YORK TIMES:
Since no one expects Hollywood to take sides, Walter Wanger's *Blockade,* which is the first fiction film to deal at all seriously with the Spanish civil war, is not to be damned for its failure to mention Loyalist and Rebel, Franco or Mussolini. If it expresses an honest hatred of war, if it deplores the bombing of civilian populations and if it closes with an appeal to the "conscience of the world," it is doing the most we can expect an American picture to do. The most, that is, from an editorial point of view. Mr. Wanger

Henry Fonda in *Blockade,* originally titled *The Rising Tide.*

has displayed rare courage in going even so far. In spite of the anonymity of his combatants, he probably will be punished for his temerity.

Courage, even in the smallest degree, is so unusual in Hollywood that we wish we could give this column's unqualified support . . . to the production of Mr. Wanger's drama. Unhappily for us all, we cannot . . . the film has a curious unreality considering the grim reality behind it. . . . The people of *Blockade* have not that [real] look: their war has been synthetic.

Already we note that the Knights of Columbus and the Catholic journals are protesting. . . .

Frank S. Nugent

NEWSWEEK:

When Walter Wanger first started the cameras grinding a film against the background of the Spanish civil war, it was ballyhooed as a powerful preachment against ruthless modern warfare, one that would take sides and name names. Immediately the international picture market began to quake; there were rumors of foreign interference with production and threatened sabotage by spies. Now the finished product, emerging as *Blockade* with a run-of-the-mill spy plot, makes one wonder what all the fuss was about. The spies either did their work well or else were wasting their time.

. . . In a closing speech to the camera's eye Henry Fonda calls on the world to end the slaughter of

Madeleine Carroll in *Blockade,* which had an original screenplay by John Howard Lawson, later blacklisted as a result of Congressional investigations into leftist leanings in Hollywood.

civilians and the starving of women and babies. But, in an effort to blend romance and propaganda into entertainment, the picture pulls its punches and falls far low of the target.

Henry Fonda and Leo Carrillo.

Linden Travers and Cecil Parker in Hitchcock's *The Lady Vanishes,* a film about the dangers of isolationist thinking and the Nazi peril.

The Lady Vanishes

Gaumont-British

New York release date, December 25, 1938

Directed by Alfred Hitchcock; screenplay by Sidney Gilliatt, Frank Launder and Alma Revelle, based on Ethel Lina White's story, "The Wheel Spins."

CAST: Margaret Lockwood, Michael Redgrave, Paul Lukas, Dame May Whitty, Cecil Parker, Linden Travers, Naughton Wayne, Basil Radford, Mary Clare, Emile Borco, Googie Withers, Sally Stewart, Philip Leaver, Zelma Vas Dias, Catherine Lacey, Josephine Wilson, Charles Oliver, Kathleen Tremaine.

This British film deserves mention here because American audiences responded nationwide to its Hitchcockian conception of Nazi villainry. Hailed by critics as a near-masterpiece of cinema derring-do, Alfred Hitchcock's superbly directed film was a cleverly contrived and suspenseful drama with Dame May Whitty as a British agent attempting to get out of Germany, running afoul of the villainous Paul Lukas, but getting assistance from Margaret Lockwood and Michael Redgrave on a trans-Europe express train.

The Lady Vanishes was the quintessential thriller, with sly undertones of propaganda about British cool versus German sloppiness in the face of crisis. Comic relief was provided by two super-British sportsman-types played to the hilt by Naughton Wayne and Basil Radford.

THE NEW YORK TIMES:

If it were not so brilliant a melodrama, we should class it as a brilliant comedy. . . . The two Englishmen aboard didn't want to be involved; they were eager to reach England in time for the cricket finals. The pacifist was afraid his reputation might suffer; he obviously was traveling with a woman not his wife. . . . There isn't an incident . . . that hasn't a pertinent bearing on the plot. . . . The man [Hitchcock] is diabolical; his film is devilishly clever.

Frank S. Nugent

NEWSWEEK:

Next to his unquestioned mastery of bated-breath suspense, Hitchcock is adept in the creation of comedy relief.

The Lady Vanishes balances its spy-and-counter-spy diet with sparkling dialogue and a pervading spirit of spoofing at England's expense. Aided by the provocative performances of an excellent cast he has turned out what is probably the most entertaining melodrama of his career.

TIME:

. . . That the elements of a Hitchcock melodrama provoke an excitement utterly lacking when the same elements are combined by less skillful directors is due to Director Hitchcock's unique talent for cinematic construction and his unparalleled experience in employing it.

Michael Redgrave and Margaret Lockwood having a drink with Paul Lukas in *The Lady Vanishes*. In this typical Hitchcock scene Lukas is attempting to drug the unsuspecting couple.

Dame May Whitty, Margaret Lockwood, Catherine Lacey, Michael Redgrave in *The Lady Vanishes*.

Confessions of a Nazi Spy

Warner Bros.

New York release date, April 28, 1939

Directed by Anatole Litvak; screenplay by Milton Krims and John Wexley, with Leon G. Turrou acting as technical adviser.

CAST: Edward G. Robinson, Francis Lederer, George Sanders, Paul Lukas, Henry O'Neill, Lya Lys, Grace Stafford, James Stephenson, Sig Rumann, Fred Tozere, Dorothy Tree, Celia Sibelius.

While this Warner Bros. film was not as sensational as its advance publicity led audiences of the day to expect, it was, nevertheless, the first out-and-out anti-Nazi film from a major American studio, sounding the alarm about spies, fifth columnists and Bundists in the United States.

The film, produced with the technical assistance of former FBI agent Leon G. Turrou, made its point by sticking closely to the facts of a real-life spy trial which had involved high officials in the Reich as well as their American operatives. It said that German consulates were little more than fronts for waging secret warfare against the United States. Although there was little in the picture that would have startled a reader of newspapers of the day, it was a powerful propaganda blast at fascist ideology and a strong pro-democracy statement. German-born Anatole Litvak directed the film with an obvious anti-Nazi

passion and a keen ear and eye for the nuances of Nazi villainy, amply provided by Francis Lederer, George Sanders, Paul Lukas and others who were ultimately undone by cool FBI man Edward G. Robinson.

This film was instrumental in bringing about the "Hollywood war-mongering" charges. Actors and producers received murder threats. American-based German officials screamed "conspiracy!" and the film was subsequently banned by countries who feared offending Germany. In the United States, however, it was a popular success, prompting other studios to hurry production of more anti-Hitler films.

NEWSWEEK:

This dramatization is a hard-hitting, sensational reminder that Hollywood is not only doctoring its local "ism"—escapism—with increasing doses of Americanism, but occasionally prescribing for the "isms" of Europe. As screen propaganda against propaganda, this Warners film pulls few haymakers.

Although actual names are not used—except in bursts of Hitler Heiling—the film omits the foreword customary in such pictures, that of branding its characters as fictional. And its principal characters are fictional in name only. Turrou, called Ed Renard, is played by Edward G. Robinson. Paul Lukas, Francis

Edward G. Robinson played a G-Man in *Confessions of a Nazi Spy.*

Lederer, George Sanders, Dorothy Tree and Lya Lys all portray actual people involved in the investigation that resulted in prison sentences for three of them.

Splendidly acted, briskly directed by Anatole Litvak, *Confessions* is vigorous, if episodic, melodrama that would seem fantastic but for its basis in fact.

THE NEW YORK TIMES:

Hitler's pledge of non-aggression toward the Americas reached the Warners too late yesterday. They had formally declared war on the Nazis at 8:15 A.M. with the first showing of their *Confessions of a Nazi Spy* at the Strand. Hitler won't like it; neither will Goebbels; frankly, we were not too favorably impressed either, although for a different reason. . . . The Warners had courage in making the picture, but we should have preferred to see them pitch their battle on a higher plane . . . [the film's] editorial bias, however justified, has carried it to several childish extremes.

The film's promised revelations have long been in the public domain, and we cannot fight down the impression that the picture has cheapened its cause and sacrificed much of its dignity by making its villains twirl their long black mustaches. (A short black one can be villainous enough.)

Frank S. Nugent

NEW YORK HERALD TRIBUNE:

The Warner Brothers, most courageous and aware of all the Hollywood studios, have turned out a compelling indictment of Nazi espionage and Nazi dogma in *Confessions of a Nazi Spy.*

. . . It is an expert piece of screen rapportage on an ugly phase of the Fascist offensive against the democracies . . . a skillfully dramatized and convincingly interpreted account of Germany's highly organized scheme to steal confidential military information from the United States, as well as its propagandistic attacks on our form of government.

. . . *Confessions of a Nazi Spy* is only a moderately exciting spy melodrama, but it is a challenging statement of opposed political philosophies and a terrible warning that democracy needs defending.

Howard Barnes

The Fighting 69th

Warner Bros.

New York release date, January 26, 1940

Directed by William Keighley; screenplay by Norman Reilly Raine, Fred Niblo Jr. and Dean Franklin.

CAST: James Cagney, Pat O'Brien, George Brent, Jeffrey Lynn, Alan Hale, Frank McHugh, Dennis Morgan, Dick Foran, William Lundigan, Guinn Williams, John Litel, Henry O'Neill, Sammy Cohen, Harvey Stephens, Charles Trowbridge, DeWolf Hopper, Tom Dugan, Frank Wilcox.

James Cagney in *The Fighting 69th*, re-released by Warner Bros. in 1948.

Warner Bros.' "inspirational" World War I martial drama came at a time when the Warners must have figured American audiences needed a bit of patriotic militarism.

James Cagney starred as a brash recruit who turns coward when he finds himself in actual combat. Pat O'Brien played the famous Father Duffy, a chaplain renowned for his battle exploits. The film traced the training of soldiers from their beginnings as unruly recruits to their term of trial in battle. Cagney of course recovered his nerve and wound up a hero.

The film was exciting and tense in its depiction of the training, the horrors of battle and as a story of the regiment. But its heroics rang false.

THE NEW YORK TIMES:

The Fighting Sixty-Ninth was having a little trouble making itself heard yesterday over the cheers and whistles of a predominantly schoolboyish audience... we don't know that we blame them altogether.

The picture is better if you can manage to forget the plot ... and think of it instead as the human, amusing and frequently gripping record of a regiment's marching off to war ... but, as the personal history of Private Plunkett and How He Became a Hero it is embarrassingly unconvincing.

And this we maintain in the face of Mr. Cagney's vivid performance of the swaggering recruit who turned yellow in the trenches, and Pat O'Brien's dignified and eloquent portrayal of the famous fighting chaplain whose monument stands in Times Square.

Frank S. Nugent

NEWSWEEK:

Based on the adventures of the New York "Irish" regiment that went overseas with the Rainbow Division as the 165th Infantry, this melodrama is highlighted by some vividly realistic war scenes and James Cagney's characterization of a two-fisted toughie who cracks under the strain of fighting an enemy he can't get his hands on. . . .

James Cagney arrives for basic training in *The Fighting 69th.*

Eugenie Leontovich with her "four sons," Don Ameche, Robert Lowery, George Ernest, Alan Curtis.

Four Sons

20th Century-Fox

New York release date, June 7, 1940

Directed by Archie Mayo; screenplay by John Howard Lawson, suggested by a story by I. A. R. Wylie.

CAST: Don Ameche, Eugenie Leontovich, Mary Beth Hughes, Alan Curtis, George Ernest, Robert Lowery, Lionel Royce, Sig Rumann, Ludwig Stossel, Christian Rub, Torben Meyer, Egon Brecher, Eleanor Wesselhoeft, Michael Visaroff, Greta Meyer, Ernst Hausman, Robert O. Davis, Hans Schumm, Fredrick Vogeding, William von Brincken, Ragnar Gvale, Robert Conway.

This heavy melodrama about a Czech family was told against the background of Nazi treachery and intrigue that ultimately overwhelmed the smaller nations of Europe. The story began before the Sudetenland crisis and ended after the fall of Warsaw. It focused on a mother (Eugenie Leontovich made her screen debut in the role) who lost three of her four sons to the monster of National Socialism. The film was an extensively revised remake of a 1928 Fox film with the same title which was set at the time of "the Great War."

Of the four sons, one goes to America to seek his fortune as an artist; one joins one of Hitler's secret fraternities and helps betray his country when the time comes; the third remains a loyal Czech and dies, along with his traitorous brother, when the Germans take over; and the fourth and youngest son joins Hitler's army and dies in Poland. The mother finally manages to leave Czechoslovakia and join her surviving son in the United States. The performances were good and the film was a sorrowful document

Eugenie Leontovich, Don Ameche, Robert Lowery, Alan Curtis, George Ernest.

of human suffering. Obviously too sorrowful, since the moviegoing public stayed away.

THE NEW YORK TIMES:
Generations come and go and the wars go on. When an earlier production of I. A. R. Wylie's *Four Sons* was released in 1928 the setting was Germany during the first World War and it was a German mother whose sons were successively sacrificed in that de-

bacle. For the current version . . . the action occurs in the Sudetenland of 1938 and the family, though of German descent, is Czech by citizenship. But there is a commentary in the fact that the stories are essentially parallel. The hearthstone is as desolate, the heart as vacant on either side of the battlelines when the sons are gone.

It is a theme rooted in the anguish of our time. . . . *Four Sons* partakes more of sentimental melodrama than of tragedy. Neither in its performance nor its

The Nazi brother, Alan Curtis, and the partisan brother, Don Ameche, confront each other.

Eugenie Leontovich, Mary Beth Hughes, Alan Curtis, Don Ameche and George Ernest in *Four Sons*.

writing does the film ever rise to any passion. . . . It never achieves a cumulative emotion.

Though *Four Sons* attempts to lay bare some of the ordeal behind the lines of today's battles, most of its emotion is stillborn. The heartbreak is largely left untold.

—*T. S.*

NEWSWEEK:

Unlike the year's previous "quickie" efforts to cash in on the current conflict, this bitter and shock-ing remake of the 1928 silent film of the same name is obviously sincere in its approach to an already dated chapter in modern history.

Whether moviegoers want war films at this time is a question producers and exhibitors have still to resolve. Although this unrelieved drama is unfolded without visiting a battlefield, the menace of guns and marching men is never very far offstage. The result is hardly entertainment; but as propaganda, *Four Sons* graphically exposes the ruthlessness of Hitler's blitzkrieg and its reliance on a Fifth Column.

Don Ameche hiding from the Nazis in *Four Sons,* produced by Darryl Zanuck, directed by Archie Mayo.

The Mortal Storm

MGM

New York release date, June 20, 1940

Directed by Frank Borzage; screenplay by Claudine West, Andresen Ellis and George Froeschel, based on the novel *The Mortal Storm* by Phyllis Bottome.

CAST: Margaret Sullavan, James Stewart, Robert Young, Frank Morgan, Robert Stack, Bonita Granville, Irene Rich, William T. Orr, Maria Ouspenskaya, Gene Reynolds, Russell Hicks, William Edmunds, Esther Dale, Dan Dailey Jr., Granville Bates, Thomas Ross, Ward Bond, Sue Moore, Harry Depp, Julius Tannen, Gus Glassmire.

Bonita Granville, James Stewart, Margaret Sullavan, Maria Ouspenskaya in *The Mortal Storm*.

Robert Young, Robert Stack, William Orr and Ward Bond hearing orders in *The Mortal Storm*.

This was MGM's version of Phyllis Bottome's novel about the tragedy Hitler's ascendancy brought to the household of a "non-Aryan" German university professor.

The professor himself, played by Frank Morgan, is eventually sent to a concentration camp. To his despair, his sons, Robert Stack and William T. Orr, become Nazis. His daughter, Margaret Sullavan, at-tempts to escape with an anti-Nazi friend, James Stewart, but is cut down just as she reaches the border. Robert Young had the unsympathetic role of a Nazi fanatic.

The Mortal Storm was sad and depressing, deriving its power from its close paralleling of personal tragedy with world-shaking events. To some contemporary observers the film seemed dated, however,

Maria Ouspenskaya, Margaret Sulla-van, James Stewart in *The Mortal Storm*.

Friends and family, including Robert Young, Margaret Sullavan and James Stewart, toast Frank Morgan in *The Mortal Storm*.

Margaret Sullavan and James Stewart find their lives threatened by National Socialism.

because of the events which had transpired from the time of its setting, 1933, to mid-1940 when it was released. By that time there was no longer any doubt about the menace in Berlin.

The film, with its unpleasant message, was a box-office failure in the United States and when it was released in Europe its anti-Nazi message caused Hitler to ban the showing of all MGM pictures in German territories.

NEW YORK HERALD TRIBUNE:

Hollywood, which has a way of being only a jump behind the headlines, is several laps behind them in the case of *The Mortal Storm* . . . [the film] is forthright in acting and projection. It calls a non-Aryan a non-Aryan and presents a sentimentally bitter commentary on those early years of Hitlerian supremacy when great books were tossed into bonfires and great liberals were flogged to death in concentration camps. For all its inherent honesty, though, the film is both dated and romantically distorted. Less than a year ago, it would have had far more dramatic and emotional impact than it has at this time. . . .

There have been a dozen plays, in my recollection,

which pointed out the terror that swept Germany when Hitler was appointed Chancellor. None of them was very convincing for the simple reason that they presupposed that there was a strong liberal sentiment in Germany which opposed the Third Reich. At this late date, this thesis may be pleasant to contemplate, but it certainly doesn't stand up factually or dramatically. . . . It is not MGM's fault but the timing on the making of *The Mortal Storm* has been extremely bad.

Howard Barnes

THE NEW YORK TIMES:

There is no use mincing words about it: *The Mortal Storm* falls definitely into the category of blistering anti-Nazi propaganda. . . . As propaganda, *The Mortal Storm* is a trumpet call to resistance, but as theatrical entertainment it is grim and depressing today.

The Mortal Storm . . . is comforting at this time only in its exposition of heroic stoicism. As the oppressed professor says, "I've never prized safety, either for myself or my children. I've prized courage."

Bosley Crowther

Foreign Correspondent

United Artists

New York release date, August 27, 1940

Produced by Walter Wanger; directed by Alfred Hitchcock; screenplay by Charles Bennett and Joan Harrison, with dialogue by James Hilton and Robert Benchley.

CAST: Joel McCrea, Laraine Day, Herbert Marshall, George Sanders, Albert Basserman, Robert Benchley, Edmund Gwenn, Harry Davenport, Eduardo Ciannelli, Martin Kosleck, Barbara Pepper, Eddie Conrad, Grauford Kent, Gertrude W. Hoffman, Jane Novak, Joan Brodel, Louis Borrell, Eily Malyon, E. E. Clive.

Joel McCrea and Albert Basserman.

Walter Wanger, whose production *Blockade* had created an international stir in 1938, produced this Alfred Hitchcock-directed suspense drama about a young American crime reporter (Joel McCrea) assigned to cover Europe. The film was a fascinating, fantastic fable combining spy plots, political assassination, hairbreadth escapes and the intrigues of international politics.

A spectacular plane crash at sea and a political assassination with a gun hidden in a camera were typical hallmarks of the Hitchcock creative genius, as was the casting of kindly, likable Edmund Gwenn as a hired killer. The film ended with McCrea, caught in the London blitz with bombs falling in the background, making a passionate plea via radio for American intervention before the lights went out all over Europe.

Foreign Correspondent had an interesting pre-production history. Producer Wanger paid newspaperman Vincent Sheean $10,000 for his book *Personal History,* set two writers to work on it, then discarded the result. He next hired John Howard Lawson to write a new script about the adventures of a U. S. newspaperman in Spain and Germany and engaged William Dieterle to direct. Before production began, the Spanish War was over. Wanger started over again, hiring two *March of Time* writers to script the story in their fashion, then he switched back to Sheean. After the Nazi invasion of Poland, Wanger turned the whole project over to Alfred Hitchcock. Hitchcock, with Charles Bennett, James Hilton, Robert Benchley and Ben Hecht evolved the final version, which, fourteen writers and $1,500,000 away from *Personal History,* had nothing to do with Sheean.

During production, Wanger constantly had scenes rewritten and reshot and spent an additional $250,000 in order to keep his film up to date with world events. Interestingly, *Foreign Correspondent* was a favorite film of Reich propaganda minister Joseph Goebbels, who saw it as a masterpiece of propaganda, "a first class production, a criminological bang-up hit, which no doubt will make a certain impression upon the broad masses of the people in enemy countries." Goebbels continued, "Significantly enough, this film, with its absolutely anti-German tendency was allowed to run for months in Sweden. The Swedes and the Swiss are playing with fire. Let us hope they will burn their fingers before the war is over."

NEW YORK HERALD TRIBUNE:

A stunning melodrama. . . . It took audacity to frame an arrant shocker in the terrible events of this terrible present, but Mr. Hitchcock and Mr. Wanger have had the nerve to do it. No punches have been pulled in describing the Gestapo or fifth columnists, while the ending of the film is as challenging a call to arms as the screen has issued to democracy. . . . This juxtaposition of outright melodramatics with deadly serious propaganda is eminently satisfactory. . . . Hitchcock uses camera tricks, cinematic rhythm and crescendo to make his points. They come over with enormous power. . . . Instead of cramping his style, Hollywood has given the director a chance to increase his stature. . . . The cast of *Foreign Correspondent* is fine, but it is Mr. Hitchcock's superb staging which makes it one of the best pictures of the year.

Howard Barnes

TIME:

. . . Easily one of the year's finest pictures. . . . Best reporter in *Foreign Correspondent* is Hitchcock's camera. When a diplomat is shot, the camera is in the right place, looking at his face. When a man is about to drop from a tower, it watches a hat making the plunge first. When a wounded Clipper is hurtling down toward the sea, it is peering anxiously from the pilot's seat. It has, too, the supreme reporter's gift of not telling everything. . . .

Charlie Chaplin as "the great dictator."

The Great Dictator

United Artists

New York release date, October 15, 1940

Written, produced and directed by Charles Chaplin.

CAST: Charles Chaplin, Jack Oakie, Reginald Gardiner, Henry Daniell, Billy Gilbert, Grace Hayle, Carter de Haven, Paulette Goddard, Maurice Moscovich, Emma Dunn, Bernard Gorcey, Paul Weigel, Chester Conklin, Esther Michelson, Hank Mann, Florence Wright, Eddie Gribbon, Robert O. Davis, Eddie Dunn, Nita Pike, Peter Lynn.

The incomparable Charlie Chaplin, heretofore the lonely little clown with baggy pants, had something more to note in this film than the funny and moving misadventures of a charming nonconformist.

Chaplin played a Jewish barber in a ghetto who recovers from amnesia and finds himself in the bewildering and frightening world of a National Socialist Germany, run by a ranting and petulant maniac dictator, Hynkel, also played by Chaplin. Jack Oakie played Napaloni, the equally recognizable dictator of a neighboring country.

The barber discovers the horrors of life under Hynkel, is beaten up and ultimately flees the country only to be mistaken for Hynkel in the recently annexed country to which he escapes. The film ends with Chaplin, as himself, making an impassioned plea for reason and brotherly love.

Although Chaplin's intention was satire, by the time the film was released Hitler had become something other than a laughing matter and the film suffered because of the turn of world events.

For his dual performance, Chaplin was voted the New York Film Critics' Best Actor award, but he rejected it because of his disappointment at the critical reaction to the film itself. The critics said that they nevertheless felt that his was the best performance of the year, that it "touched a high mark in his career, and matched the perfection expected of him by his enormous public."

NEWSWEEK:

This, I regret to say, is not a great Chaplin picture, although there are a few flashes of Chaplin the Great.... We have all read too much about the murderous pouts of Hitler, when his yes-men do not yes, to see anything funny in sending to a concentration camp an aviator who suggests more temperate treatment of the Jews. Furthermore, Jews are called Jews in this picture, and there certainly is nothing funny about what are undoubtedly word-for-word sentences of further persecution of the race. No time for comedy? Yes, I say time for comedy. Time for Chaplin comedy. No time ever for Chaplin to preach as he does those last six minutes, no matter how deeply he may feel what he wrote and says. He is not a good preacher. Indeed, he is frighteningly bad.

John O'Hara

Chaplin as Hynkel, Henry Daniell and Jack Oakie as Napaloni.

Reginald Gardiner and Charlie Chaplin.

THE NEW YORK TIMES:

The prospect of little "Charlot," the most universally loved character in all the world, directing his superlative talent for ridicule against the most dangerously evil man alive has loomed as a titanic jest, a transcendent paradox. And the happy result this morning is that it comes off magnificently. . . . It is as the dictator that Chaplin displays his true genius. Whatever fate it was that decreed Adolf Hitler should look like Charlie must have ordained this opportunity, for the caricature of the former is devastating. . . . All the vulnerable spots of Hitler's exterior are pierced by Chaplin's pantomimic shafts. He is at his best in a wild senseless burst of guttural oratory—a compound of German, Yiddish and Katzenjammer double-talk; and he reaches positively exalted heights in a plaintive dance which he does with a large balloon representing the globe, bouncing it into the air, pirouetting beneath it and then bursting into tears when the balloon finally pops. . . .

On the debit side, the picture is overlong, it is inclined to be repetitious and the speech with which it ended—the appeal for reason and kindness—is completely out of joint with that which has gone before.

Bosley Crowther

Paulette Goddard gets a haircut from the mild-mannered barber, Charlie Chaplin, who is a double for the dictator.

NEW YORK HERALD TRIBUNE:

Were it not for the terrible events of the last year, this caricature of the madman in Europe might have had telling propagandistic as well as comic effect. . . . With almost surgical precision, Chaplin lays a monster bare, with all his monstrous foibles, before one. . . . Moreover, when Chaplin steps out of it at the end in a challenging call to arms, even its satirical quality becomes diffused. . . .

Howard Barnes

Charlie Chaplin in his classic pose as "the great dictator."

Escape

MGM

New York release date, October 31, 1940

Produced and directed by Mervyn LeRoy; screenplay by Arch Oboler and Marguerite Roberts, based on the novel by Ethel Vance.

CAST: Norma Shearer, Robert Taylor, Conrad Veidt, Nazimova, Felix Bressart, Albert Bassermann, Philip Dorn, Bonita Granville, Edgar Barrier, Elsa Bassermann, Blanche Yurka.

Mervyn LeRoy produced and directed MGM's adaptation of the controversial 1939 best-seller by Ethel Vance (a pseudonym). The film dealt with the outspoken American son of a German actress, who goes to Germany (in the book the locale was not precisely identified) to find his mother and discovers that she is imprisoned in a concentration camp and scheduled for execution. The son, played by Robert Taylor, then begins a frantic effort to free her and get her out of the country. He enlists the aid of a doctor in the concentration camp and is able to smuggle his mother out and hide her in the home of an American-

Conrad Veidt, Norma Shearer in *Escape*. Veidt became the quintessential Nazi officer in films of the war years.

born countess, played by Norma Shearer. He ultimately is able to spirit her out of the country just before Hitler begins his annexations under the *lebensraum* program.

Silent-screen star Alla Nazimova made her talking-picture debut as the actress in this suspenseful anti-Nazi melodrama. Whereas the novelist had been vague about identifying the locale of the story, the moviemakers pulled no punches and didn't hesitate to indicate Germany as the totalitarian country and the Nazis as the villains.

Hitler was infuriated by *Escape* and threatened to ban all MGM films from Reich-controlled markets. When the foreign release of *The Mortal Storm* added more insult to his injury, the ban was immediately implemented.

NEW YORK HERALD TRIBUNE:

The film is even more specific in its anti-Nazi stand than the [novel]. It documents the terror of totali-

Robert Taylor and Norma Shearer.

Germany and warns him that it will be different when he is in his own back yard. It is just as well, though, that MGM was intent on showmanship as well as propaganda. . . . The supporting players make *Escape* a compelling exhibit . . . Alla Nazimova . . . is splendid as the actress.

Howard Barnes

THE NEW YORK TIMES:

This is far and away the most dramatic and hair-raising picture yet made on the sinister subject of persecution in a totalitarian land. . . . Propaganda? Well, of course—if you choose to label a picture which tells a documented story with that word. . . .

Bosley Crowther

Robert Taylor.

Nazimova, Robert Taylor, and Norma Shearer.

tarian existence in the months that preceded the second World War with powerful emphasis . . . [it is] striking entertainment as well as an indictment of a system. . . .

. . . The motion picture has plenty of opportunity to do some savage editorializing on the Nazi ideology . . . castigating the new Hunnish onslaught on civilization. . . .

I applaud the references to the present world crisis, as when the American youngster turns on the overbearing general who has told him to get out of

Veronica Lake and Ray Milland in
I Wanted Wings.

I Wanted Wings

Paramount

New York release date, March 26, 1941

Produced by Arthur Hornblow, Jr.; directed by Mitchell Leisen; screenplay by Richard Maibaum, Lieut. Beirne Lay, Jr. and Sig Herzig, based on a story by Eleanore Griffin and Frank Wead from the book *I Wanted Wings,* by Beirne Lay, Jr.

CAST: Ray Milland, William Holden, Wayne Morris, Brian Donlevy, Constance Moore, Veronica Lake, Harry Davenport, Phil Brown, Edward Fielding, Willard Robertson, Richard Lane, Addison Richards, Hobart Cavanaugh, Douglas Aylesworth,

Ray Milland, Brian Donlevy, Wayne Morris, and William Holden.

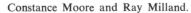
Constance Moore and Ray Milland.

Ray Milland and buddies.

Ray Milland and Wayne Morris.

John Trent, Archie Twitchell, Richard Webb, John Hiestand.

Filmed on location at Randolph and Kelly Fields near San Antonio, Texas, with the cooperation of the Army Air Corps, Paramount's aerial epic followed the personal lives and training of three young men—a wealthy playboy (Ray Milland), a college athlete (Wayne Morris), and an automobile mechanic (William Holden)—as they went through aviation school hoping to earn their wings and be commissioned in the Air Corps.

Mitchell Leisen directed Ray Milland in *I Wanted Wings*.

The film company reached Randolph Field at the same time as a new batch of cadets arrived and the producer matched the progress of his three fictional airmen with the training pace of the student pilots.

While the aerial sequences were stunningly effective, the film was grounded by stock romantic subplots involving a lady photographer (Constance Moore) and a blond siren (the screen debut of Veronica Lake) who complicated the boys' lives, muddled the progress of their training, and damaged the credibility of the film. *I Wanted Wings* did, however, sound the bugle about the "beautiful Army Air Corps" and was undoubtedly responsible for more than a few enlistments.

NEW YORK HERALD TRIBUNE:

I Wanted Wings has a lot of stirring and provocative aviation excitement to recommend it. Particularly fine, to my mind, is the section in which Los Angeles is blacked out in a terrible forecast of the possible shape of things to come. As a personal, dramatic entertainment, it leaves so much to be desired that it must be set down as a faltering screen show.

Howard Barnes

TIME:

. . . When it sticks to flying, *I Wanted Wings* offers educational and tingling entertainment along with some of the cinema's best aviation photography. Elsewhere, Paramount's picture of life in the air force resembles a mixture of West Point and Minsky's.

Vivien Leigh as "that Hamilton woman."

That Hamilton Woman

United Artists

New York release date, April 3, 1941

Produced and directed by Alexander Korda; screenplay by Walter Reisch and R. C. Sherriff.

CAST: Vivien Leigh, Laurence Olivier, Alan Mowbray, Sara Allgood, Gladys Cooper, Henry Wilcoxon, Heather Angel, Halliwell Hobbes, Gilbert Emery, Miles Mander, Ronald Sonclair, Luis Alberni, Norma Drury, Olaf Hytten, Juliette Compton, Guy Kingsford.

Produced and directed in Hollywood by Alexander Korda, *That Hamilton Woman* was, on one level, the story of Britain's famous lovers, Admiral Lord Nelson (Laurence Olivier) and Emma, Lady Hamilton (Vivien Leigh). On another level it was an eloquent and moving testament to British resolve in the face of adversity, and was effective pro-British propaganda, fostering strong feelings for the embattled nation.

The story was set against the background of the British war with the French. The film traced the touching Nelson-Hamilton romance from the time Emma became the wife of Lord Hamilton through her years with Nelson until his death while defending England against Napoleon's fleet in the Battle of Trafalgar.

That Hamilton Woman was Sir Winston Churchill's favorite movie and he had it screened many times.

NEWSWEEK:

... Strains for analogies between England's present fight and the war with the "dictator" Napoleon. ... Vivien Leigh is notably successful in making Emma as vivacious and fascinating as she must have been;

but Olivier, although he scowls heavily and sacrifices an eye and an arm to impersonate Nelson, is hard to believe as the heroic sea dog.

THE NEW YORK TIMES:

Now that the spirit of Nelson is again at large upon the deep and the expectations of England are being triumphantly fulfilled, it is altogether fitting that the greatest Admiral ever to lead a British fleet, at this moment should be pictured with profound affection and respect upon the screen. . . . It is the glory of Nelson which the film most devotedly extols. Lady Hamilton exists because of his interest in her. . . . In short, the whole film is just a running account of a famous love affair, told with deep sympathy for the participants against a broad historic outline of the times. . . . As a memorial to a "great little man" and his tortured life, *That Hamilton Woman* leaves much to be desired. But coming at a moment such as this, it should stir any one's interest. . . .

Bosley Crowther

Vivien Leigh and Laurence Olivier played the classic lovers, Lord Nelson and Lady Hamilton.

Vivien Leigh and Laurence Olivier in *That Hamilton Woman,* a favorite propaganda film in Britain.

Walter Pidgeon pursued by the Nazis in *Man Hunt.*

Man Hunt

20th Century-Fox

New York release date, June 13, 1941

Produced by Kenneth MacGowan, directed by Fritz Lang; screenplay by Dudley Nichols, based on the novel *Rogue Male,* by Geoffrey Household.

CAST: Walter Pidgeon, Joan Bennett, George Sanders, John Carradine, Roddy McDowall, Heather Thatcher, Frederick Worlock, Roger Imhof, Egon Brecher, Lester Matthews, Holmes Herbert, Eily Malyon, Arno Frey, Fredrik Vogeding, Lucien Prival, Herbert Evans, Keith Hitchcock.

Although he was offered the directorship of Germany's film industry by Reichminister Joseph Goebbels, director Fritz Lang left Germany and came to the United States, where he was signed by 20th Century-Fox. Lang's first film for Fox was *Man Hunt,* based on Geoffrey Household's best seller, *Rogue Male.* It was the story of a Britisher, portrayed by

Walter Pidgeon, who goes to Germany before the war and, purely for sport, stalks Hitler with a rifle. When he has the dictator in his sights he debates with himself whether to shoot, but is captured by the Gestapo, who attempt to use him in an international intrigue. Pidgeon escapes and is pursued by Gestapo agents who follow him back to England.

Joan Bennett provided the romantic interest as a streetwalker who saves Pidgeon's life. George Sanders was perfect as the Gestapo chief. The film itself was a compelling and bitter comment on the social and ideological atmosphere in Hitler's Germany.

THE NEW YORK TIMES:

A great many folks in the world have toyed fondly with the dream of taking a pot shot at Hitler from some convenient blind. . . . If you are one of the people who have entertained that desperate thought,

48

Heather Thatcher and Joan Bennett.

Walter Pidgeon struggles with his pursuer, John Carradine.

you shouldn't miss this film. For it tells of an English big-game hunter who, shortly before the outbreak of the present war, conceives the fantastic notion of simply stalking Hitler for sport. . . . For its keen and vivid contrast of British and Nazi temperaments, its interesting analysis of the so-called sportsman's code, *Man Hunt* rates somewhat above the run of ordinary "chase" films. . . . Exciting? Yes, it is. But convincing? No. Somehow you just keep on asking, "For

goodness sake, what makes Captain Thorndike [Walter Pidgeon] run?"

Bosley Crowther

NEW YORK HERALD TRIBUNE:

. . . Considerably more than a fabulous melodrama. . . . The whole democratic point of view receives stirring statement in the hero's stoical defiance of his captors and his final death struggle with a ruthless Gestapo chief. . . . The German military and espionage system is savagely caricatured in several sequences. . . . The scenarist has kept his German characters talking German to other Germans, which may be a slight novelty but adds a great deal to the conviction of the narrative. . . . The expatriated German director [Fritz Lang] has never failed to give a passage of *Man Hunt* exciting and explicit statement. Until the ending, which devolves into a rather anticlimactic series of montage effects. . . .

Howard Barnes

Gestapo chief George Sanders has plans for Walter Pidgeon in *Man Hunt*.

Joan Bennett helps Walter Pidgeon escape.

Dorothy Lamour makes army life bearable for Bob Hope and Eddie Bracken.

Caught in the Draft

Paramount

New York release date, June 25, 1941

Produced by B. G. De Sylva, directed by David Butler; screenplay by Harry Tugend.

CAST: Bob Hope, Dorothy Lamour, Lynne Overman, Eddie Bracken, Clarence Kolb, Paul Hurst, Ferike Boros, Phyllis Ruth, Irving Bacon, Arthur Loft, Edgar Dearing.

Coming months before the Japanese attack on Pearl Harbor, at a time when draft evasion was still the stuff from which laughs might be milked, *Caught in the Draft* gave Bob Hope one of his best and funniest roles as a Hollywood star trying various ruses to beat the Selective Service system. Needless to say, Hope was hooked when one of his schemes backfired. His induction into an army camp and subsequent misadventures as a gun-shy ex-star who faints at the sight of blood, brought laughter to American audiences. And the film was, in its way, a very effective flag-waver.

Appearing with Hope were Dorothy Lamour as a colonel's daughter with whom Hope falls in love; Lynne Overman, in a hilarious supporting role as Hope's agent and Eddie Bracken as Hope's girl-crazy valet who follows his boss into the army, along with the agent, whose percentage of Hope's service pay wouldn't be enough to support him. Hilarious situations and dialogue abounded, and Hope wound up both a hero and a bridegroom.

THE NEW YORK TIMES:

. . . If you are looking for some fun [watch] . . . Bob

Pampered movie star Bob Hope arrives with his valet, Eddie Bracken, to begin basic training in *Caught in the Draft*.

Hope, the most persistently perplexed man on the screen, tearing himself to pieces, all because of the Selective Service Act. . . . Mark it down on your list as something to be seen on the day that you (or your boy-friend) get that summons to report. It will make you feel much better. . . . Every now and then, Old Glory snaps triumphantly in the breeze, and you sense that *Caught in the Draft* will serve as something more than a lark. . . .

Bosley Crowther

NEW YORK HERALD TRIBUNE:

. . . The smart and saucy dialogue, with its innuendoes and topical allusions, is tailor-made for the comedian's rapid-fire type of delivery, and each situation is a broad burlesque of the immediate subject at hand, be it Hollywood, the Army or love. . . . It is heartening to find so much good-natured fun in a film touching on a vital defense unit. *Caught in the Draft* is broad comedy at its very best.

Robert W. Dana

Joe Sawyer, Gary Cooper, George
Tobias in *Sergeant York*.

Sergeant York

Warner Bros.

New York release date, July 2, 1941

Produced by Jesse L. Lasky and Hal B. Wallis;
directed by Howard Hawks; screenplay by Abem
Finkel, Harry Chandlee, Howard Koch and John
Huston; based on the diary of Sergeant Alvin C.
York.

CAST: Gary Cooper, Walter Brennan, Joan Leslie,
Stanley Ridges, George Tobias, Ward Bond, Margaret Wycherly, June Lockhart, Noah Beery, Jr.,
Clem Bevans, Charles Trowbridge, David Bruce, Joseph Sawyer, Robert Porterfield, Erville Alderson.

Warner Bros. assembled its top-line talent for the
stirring patriotic story of the Tennessee hillbilly who
was America's number one hero in the First World
War, having captured 132 Germans singlehandedly
in the Argonne in October 1918. This exceedingly
faithful film biography traced the life of York from
his early boisterous years through his conversion to a
deeply religious pacifist who underwent a great personal mental struggle before reluctantly deciding that
he had to fight for his country. The film ended with
York returning to his Tennessee farm after the war.

Making it the condition upon which he would consent for the film to be made, the real Alvin York
requested that Gary Cooper portray him on the
screen. Cooper won the Academy Award and New
York Film Critics Award for his performance.

Gary Cooper played the real-life Alvin York in the screen
biography of the American World War I hero.

51

Sergeant York was a moving and important film for Americans who, in 1941, were trying to make up their minds about what role the country should play in the raging European conflict.

THE NEW YORK TIMES:

At this time, when a great many people are thinking deep and sober thoughts about the possible involvement of our country in another deadly world war, Warner Bros. . . . have reflected upon the motives and influences which inspired America's No. 1 hero in the last war. . . . The first . . . phase of the picture is rich. The manner in which York is persuaded to join the fighting forces and the scenes of actual combat betray an unfortunate artificiality, however—in the battle scenes, especially—and the overly glamorized ending in which York returns to a spotless little farm, jars sharply with the naturalness which has gone before. The suggestion of deliberate propaganda is readily detected here . . . the performance of Gary Cooper in the title role holds the picture together magnificently and even the most unfavorable touches are made palatable because of him.

Bosley Crowther

NEW YORK HERALD TRIBUNE:

. . . To the great credit of Warner Bros., no short cuts have been taken to capture public response. *Sergeant York* is the tale of a strangely typical American . . . a stirring saga of Southern hill folk as well as a call to arms. . . . The photoplay handles York's inherent horror of killing with splendid restraint and dramatic effectiveness, showing him as a hero who only wanted to stop guns from killing

Gary Cooper as Sergeant York.

people. It might have been a specious apologia for a war picture, but as it stands, it gives rare substance to the eulogy of a famous soldier.

Howard Barnes

TIME:

. . . A story of an American country boy and how he came to fight for his country. . . . When war comes, he is teaching a Sunday school class. His conscientious objections ("War's ag'in the Book") are overcome by his superior officer and the history of the United States. York decides there are times when a man has no choice but to fight for his country.

Walter Brennan and Joan Leslie are among the home folks who turn out to welcome their hero.

Errol Flynn, Fred MacMurray and Regis Toomey in *Dive Bomber.*

Dive Bomber

Warner Bros.

New York release date, August 29, 1941

Directed by Michael Curtiz; screenplay by Frank Wead and Robert Buckner, from a story by Frank Wead.

CAST: Errol Flynn, Fred MacMurray, Ralph Bellamy, Alexis Smith, Robert Armstrong, Regis Toomey, Allen Jenkins, Craig Stevens, Herbert Anderson, Moroni Olsen, Dennie Moore, Louis Jean Heydt, Cliff Nazarro.

Made with the assistance of the United States Navy, Warner Bros.' *Dive Bomber* was an exciting film basically concerned with aviation medicine. It told a story of the medical men practicing and experi-

menting in the field and the pilots who were their patients and guinea pigs. Errol Flynn was his usual dashing self as a young Naval surgeon who decided to devote himself to aviation medicine after an injured pilot died on his operating table during surgery. The film itself was physically beautiful, with many masterfully photographed and engrossing sequences both in the air and in the laboratory. It was a fitting salute to a group of dedicated men who were charting new paths in medical knowledge.

THE NEW YORK TIMES:

. . . Never before has an aviation film been so vivid in its images. . . . And the story? Well, again we face a necessary evil . . . the old Hollywood notion that no man can be a hero (or a genius) without first being misunderstood. . . . In the few glimpses we have of her Alexis Smith looks good; can't tell you yet how she acts.

But chief credit for the glory that's in this picture goes to the United States Navy, which cooperated in its production and to the fellows who aimed the cameras. They collectively gave it powerful and steady wings.

Bosley Crowther

Fred MacMurray.

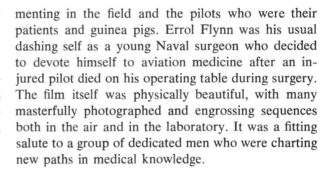

John Sutton, Tyrone Power's competition for Betty Grable's favors in *A Yank in the RAF*.

A Yank in the RAF

20th Century-Fox

New York release date, September 26, 1941

Produced by Darryl F. Zanuck; directed by Henry King; screenplay by Darrell Ware and Karl Tunberg, based on an original story by Melville Crossman.

CAST: Tyrone Power, Betty Grable, John Sutton, Reginald Gardiner, Donald Stuart, John Wilde, Richard Fraser, Bruce Lester, Gilchrist Stuart, Denis Green, Stuart Robertson, Lester Matthews, Frederick Worlock, Claud Allister, John Rogers, Ethel Griffies, John Hartley, Eric Lonsdale, Alphonse Martell, Hans von Morhart, Lilyan Irene.

This strongly pro-British drama from 20th Century-Fox was concocted by studio chief Darryl Zanuck. To insure box-office success, Zanuck used his top stars, Tyrone Power and Betty Grable, in the leading roles. Power played an American flyer who was hired to deliver a bomber to England. While there, he joins

Tyrone Power was "a Yank in the RAF."

Tyrone Power and Betty Grable.

the RAF and meets and falls in love with American dancer Grable.

There were excellent sequences, such as a leaflet bombing mission on Berlin before the fall of France, and the forced landing of a bomber in Holland, placing Power and his wing commander only a few suspenseful steps ahead of the advancing German army.

The film reached its climax with an effectively restaged evacuation of Dunkerque, with special emphasis on the role played by the RAF in making the strategic retreat possible.

Zanuck, as mentioned earlier, was one of the studio heads in favor of American intervention in the war between England and Germany. In the original script

Wounded British fighters are rescued.

The poster for *A Yank in the RAF* emphasized the authenticity of its sky battles as well as Betty Grable's glamour.

for the film, the American flyer was killed in a German air raid. The British requested, however, that the ending be changed to let Tyrone Power live. Apparently they didn't want to give American moviegoers the impression that Americans helping Britain would die. One can speculate, too, that the film might not have been the huge success it was, had Power's character died instead of winding up with Betty Grable.

NEW YORK HERALD TRIBUNE:

Isolationists will doubtless be horrified by the new film at the Roxy. *A Yank in the RAF* not only admits that there is a war being waged, but it takes sides very frankly with the gallant British airmen who saved a fragment of Europe for democracy a year ago . . . Hollywood might as well close up shop if it cannot deal with a few realities of the present day. In such a conventional adventure-romance as *A Yank in the RAF* the war gives dramatic impact and significance to a rather tawdry tale.

. . . It is neither imaginative nor conventionally captivating. What makes *A Yank in the RAF* a rather stunning entertainment is the fact that it keys right into memorable events which constitute the pattern of this present chapter in history.

. . . *A Yank in the RAF* may be warmongering. That is what makes it a worthwhile screen entertainment.

Howard Barnes

56

The War Years: 1942-1945

There are probably as many stories about Hollywood during the war years as there were people employed there, and every war movie has its own history. It would be as impossible to tell all the stories as it would be to know all of them. There were undoubtedly countless heroes whose hymns shall remain unsung, but their accomplishments and contributions are nevertheless undiminished. To contend that what we tell here is the entire story would be foolish simply because the entire story is so vast that no one volume, nor a dozen, could tell it all. But a lot of the story of Hollywood's role in wartime is, we think, told in the films of World War II, in what they were, how they were made, and what people thought of them.

The story is told in terms of the writers, directors, producers, stars and thousands of technicians who toiled and gave Rosie the Riveter, at home, and lonesome G.I.s in the Sahara night, a few minutes away from the assembly line and the pressures of combat to watch Van Johnson carry the war home to the Japanese in *Thirty Seconds Over Tokyo* or Betty Grable cheer up the boys in uniform in *Pin Up Girl*.

After Pearl Harbor, Hollywood tooled up to produce war propaganda just as Detroit tooled up to produce tanks and jeeps. Between 1942 and 1944 about 375 of the films produced in Hollywood were clearly propagandistic There was no longer any necessity for pussyfooting where fascism was concerned, and the accusations of "war-mongering" were heard no more.

The immediate concern was how Hollywood and its personnel could help the war effort. There were many ways, as we have seen, in addition to producing films, and Hollywood always gave the best that it could offer. The film industry used its enormous resources and facilities to produce thousands of films, documentaries, training films, newsreels, war propaganda and pure escapist entertainment.

The war brought a number of production problems, however, and the industry found itself having to cut back on location shooting and travel because of gas and tire rationing. Expenditures on set construction were curtailed, and the wartime shortage of materials prompted the studios to cooperate and swap some major set constructions.

Censorship also became a nuisance, if not exactly a problem, since no studio would have knowingly turned out any product that would have been detrimental to the Allied cause. Soon after the war began, President Franklin Roosevelt appointed Lowell Mellett to coordinate film production. Mellett was personally opposed to censorship and had hoped to avoid it, but censorship was ordered for all films that would be exported or imported, which in effect applied to every major film in production, since the studios exported to foreign markets.

The Pentagon also exercised control over the films to which it lent assistance. All films about the Army, Navy or Army Air Corps had to be cleared by the War Department, where the script was read before the official okay was given.

"Motion pictures are as necessary to the men as

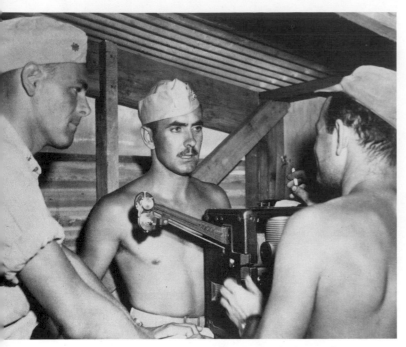

Serviceman Tyrone Power, usually in front of cameras, learns a few things about projectors.

There were other restrictions, including a limit on the number of prints of a film that could be made. The number was set at 285 release prints, which caused a backlog of films waiting to be released. In addition, the government levied a 20% admission tax on theater tickets. But even with these restrictions film production continued apace and the industry prospered as movie attendance climbed and the demand for new films increased.

Films about the war itself were important in two respects: first, they quenched a tremendous public thirst for information about the war; and second, they did an enormous job of morale boosting, showing audiences their sons and husbands and lovers in action and offering war industry workers vivid evidence of the importance of the arms and equipment they were manufacturing.

Along with the many fictional war films Hollywood produced, there were many feature-length documen-

rations," said Major General Charles H. Bonesteel in response to a question about the importance of movies to the war effort. With this in mind, the government gave considerable assistance to Hollywood for the production of movies about the war, even though the troops themselves preferred pure entertainment over what they often considered "tin-horn" Hollywood heroics. As a result of the War Department's aid, war movies of a scope never before known were made.

Dore Schary, who supervised the production of several war films, recalls the government's role: "Once we got into the war the government opened up everything that we needed. We got technical advisers, we were able to go into army camps to shoot the guys; we were able to get the armed forces assistance in terms of soldiers to simulate warfare or help with training actors who were portraying soldiers, and we got the use of Army, Navy and Air Force equipment. We got very good cooperation."

But the cooperation did not come without a price tag, and scripts had to be submitted to an office in the Pentagon for approval. While censorship *per se* was not practiced, as Schary recalls, "they'd say 'we'd rather you not do that' or 'that doesn't sound right.'" Cooperation was withheld unless changes were made.

The admiration seems to be mutual as Barbara Stanwyck signs autographs for a group of obviously delighted G.I.s.

Bette Davis promoted the American Red Cross.

taries about the war. Among the best was *The True Glory*, produced by England's Captain Carol Reed and America's Captain Garson Kanin. It traced the history of the Allied European campaign from the Normandy invasion to V-E Day, with the emphasis on the cooperative nature of the Allied war effort. Every nationality that took part in the drive to Berlin was represented in the film, which described history through the eyes of the men and women who were making it.

Another very good documentary was *The Fighting Lady*, produced by the U. S. Navy and 20th Century-Fox. It chronicled the career of an aircraft carrier from her launching through a number of battles, in scenes of violent action and visual magnificence. These films, with others such as *The Memphis Belle, With the Marines at Tarawa, The Battle of Midway, At the Front in North Africa, Attack! The Battle for New Britain, The Battle for the Marianas* and *The Liberation of Rome* comprise a stunning filmic record of the Allied ordeal and the struggle toward

the ultimate hard-won victory. Despite their overall excellence, none of these films was successful at the box office. Wartime movie audiences preferred fiction to fact.

Even the non-battle fiction was, however, marked by the turmoil of the times. Programmers and series such as Tarzan, Sherlock Holmes, Maisie, Charlie Chan and Abbott and Costello pictures turned up with plot elements related to the war. Among these films were *Tarzan Triumphs, Maisie Gets Her Man* and *Swing-Shift Maisie* (with Ann Sothern as the ever-rampant blonde cutie), *Buck Privates* (with Abbott and Costello in service—and the audiences in stitches), *Sherlock Holmes and the Voice of Terror* and *Sherlock Holmes and the Secret Weapon* (which found the Arthur Conan Doyle character updated and involved with Axis antagonists and espionage), and even the inscrutable Oriental detective turned up in *Charlie Chan Joins the Secret Service.*

With many war pictures on the agenda, Hollywood had to look hard to find enough Oriental and Teutonic types to cast as "the enemy." Top movie Nazis included Paul Lukas, Conrad Veidt, Peter Lorre, Hans Schumm, Judith Anderson, Signe Hasso, Erich von Stroheim, Basil Rathbone, Lee J. Cobb, Tala Birell, Sig Rumann, George Sanders, Walter Slezak, Raymond Massey, Otto Kruger, Francis Lederer, Martin Kosleck, Otto Preminger, William von Brincken and Sydney Greenstreet, who worked both the German and Japanese sides of the Axis street.

Among the "yellow peril" were Benson Fong, H. T. Tsiang, Noel Madison, Philip Ahn, Richard Loo, and countless Chinese extras. Chinese were used in Japanese parts because almost all Japanese-Americans had been placed in internment camps after the attack on Pearl Harbor, as a precaution against espionage and sabotage.

It is interesting in retrospect to see how "the enemy" was portrayed. The Germans were invariably portrayed as cultured swine; they could be brutal, but were intellectual about it all. The Japanese, on the other hand were presented as fanatical near-savages, sneaky, dirty fighters. Early in the war Hollywood's movie references to the Japanese as "yellow cowards" and "yellow rats" ("yellow bastards" was taboo in those Hays-office days) caused some official nervousness in Washington where the Office of War Information pointed out to the producers that the Chinese were our allies and they were yellow, too, and might not like the racial slurs implicit in such language. Hollywood agreed and the Japanese became just plain cowards, rats—and savages.

In light of the differences in the way Germans and Japanese were depicted—and the Japanese were al-

59

Airmen James Stewart and Clark Gable both saw plenty of enemy action during distinguished careers in the Army Air Corps.

ways more brutal, indulging in torture and rape to excess, and with obvious pleasure—it seems strange to note that Americans in postwar years seem to have gotten over their animosity toward the Japanese much more readily than with regard to the Germans, to whom we are much closer related in many respects.

As a result of the rise of the Nazis in Germany and the subsequent occupation of Europe, Hollywood became the home of a number of refugee directors, including Henry Koster, Ernst Lubitsch, William Dieterle and Fritz Lang from Germany and Rene Clair and Jean Renoir from France. During the war Lang made four films about the Nazis: *Man Hunt, Hangmen Also Die, Ministry of Fear* and *Cloak and Dagger.* Renoir made *This Land Is Mine,* which dealt with the German occupation of France; Lubitsch made *To Be or Not to Be,* and Dieterle directed *Blockade* in 1938.

All Hollywood studios were engaged in producing for the war effort, even Walt Disney, whose studio turned out numerous training, morale-boosting, documentary and patriotic animated films such as *The New Spirit,* in which Donald Duck induced people to pay income taxes, etc.; *Get in the Scrap,* with Donald in a scrap metal collection drive; *Der Fuehrer's Face,* with Donald; and *Victory Through Air Power,* an excellent documentary describing the role of the Air Corps in the war effort.

A number of prime "Americana" morale-boosting films were made during the war years which avoided battles but nevertheless carried strong patriotic messages. *Meet Me in St. Louis, Thank Your Lucky Stars, Thousands Cheer* and *Star Spangled Rhythm* were among the most popular and successful.

During the last eighteen months of the war, war-oriented features declined in number for several reasons. Production of the films became more complicated and expensive—costs ran between $1 and $2 million (large budgets in the early 40s) even with government cooperation, and that cooperation involved satisfying more and more government agencies; the productions involved a lot of shooting time, tying up studio equipment and personnel, usually in expensive location work; and, the most compelling reason, the movie-going public had become satiated with war stories. Even before 1944 exhibitors had urged the studios to give them more musicals and escapist entertainment films, when the public began to tire of hearing about the war. War films also suffered a decline in popularity as the casualties began to mount.

The public signalled its changing mood by making *Going My Way,* with Bing Crosby, a $7 million-dollar-grossing hit in 1944 and turning out in similar fashion in 1945 for *The Bells of St. Mary's,* with Crosby again playing a priest, in a film which outgrossed its predecessor by a million dollars.

As a result of Allied victories and advances in Europe American industrial production slumped as workers felt the war was coming to an end. In order to stress the importance of a continued "battle posture" in war material production, Hollywood turned out a morale-boosting film entitled *The War Speeds Up,* which resulted in a spurt in industrial output. Similarly there was another slump after Germany surrendered in May 1945, so another film, *Target—Japan,* was made to emphasize that the fight was not over and that much work lay ahead.

During the last six months of the war films appeared which treated the war in more realistic and less escapist terms. Films like *Objective Burma, A Walk in the Sun* and *The Story of G.I. Joe* approached the war with more honesty than had any before. Earlier in the war this would have been as unthinkable as having Tyrone Power die instead of getting Betty Grable at the end of *A Yank in the RAF*. Also during the closing months of the war Darryl Zanuck's lavish production *Wilson* appeared, with its careful consideration of American ideals, of the President who so hoped he could make a lasting contribution to world peace and who saw his hopes dashed when the United States rejected a role in the League of Nations. *Wilson* seemed to be a propaganda piece for the United Nations in the context of a topnotch American story.

The Clock, with Judy Garland and Robert Walker, described the difficulties war imposes on young lovers whose lives are disrupted by the demands of war and military service.

Before talking about the top films of the war years, it's worthwhile to note some favorite films of the men in uniform. In February 1943, *Newsweek* reported that the most popular films with the Army were *Wake Island, Pride of the Yankees* (the Lou Gehrig story), *To the Shores of Tripoli* (a tribute to the Marines), *Son of Fury, Sergeant York, Tortilla Flat, Captains of the Clouds, Johnny Eager, The Black Swan* and *Song of the Islands.* Additionally popular were such song-leg-and-dance pictures as *The Fleet's In, Ship Ahoy* and the Hope-Crosby-Lamour opus, *Road to Morocco. Newsweek* noted that *Mrs. Miniver* failed to place even on the runner-up list.

It all may depend on which newsmagazines you read; a year later, in 1944 *Time* reported that "G.I.s like musical comedies best, comedies next best, then adventure films and melodramas." And "without exception, G.I.s most dislike tinhorn war and homefront heroics. . . . Among war films only the Army's *Why We Fight* series and *Screen Magazine,* a newsreel, are generally liked. But *Destination Tokyo* has earned a certain respect, and *A Guy Named Joe* is well thought of in India. . . . But there is nothing friendly about G.I. reactions to films which make the enemy look stupid or easily beaten. In Rome a G.I. said: 'Stuff like Humphrey Bogart whipping a whole German armored-car column practically singlehanded gives us pains in the pratt because that kind of crap gives the folks at home the wrong kind of idea about what we are up against.' In the South Pasific as one cinema hero mowed down the enemy like Superman at harvest time, G.I.s sprang to their feet yelling:

The incomparable Marlene Dietrich was a favorite and untiring entertainer of the troops.

'Wait a minute buddy, I'll help yah!' Then they shot up the screen. But good & bad, old & new, movies are indispensable to G.I.s. One put it simply: 'Without movies we'd go nuts.' "

And during the planning for the Normandy invasion in 1944, General Dwight Eisenhower requested, "Let's have more motion pictures."

Although president and co-founder (with John Garfield) of the Hollywood Canteen, Bette Davis found time while in New York to serve in the Stage Door Canteen as well.

Barry Nelson and Laraine Day.

A Yank on the Burma Road

MGM

New York release date, January 28, 1942

Produced by Samuel Marx; directed by George B. Saitz; screenplay by George Kahn, Hugo Butler and David Lang.

CAST: Laraine Day, Barry Nelson, Stuart Crawford, Keye Luke, Sen Yung, Phillip Ahn, Knox Manning, Matthew Boulton.

A Yank on the Burma Road opened in New York City only seven weeks after the Japanese attack on Pearl Harbor. It was essentially a story about truck convoys which reach their destination despite all obstacles. It turned primarily around the experiences of a stalwart American (Barry Nelson) whose main interests are money and publicity. Nelson, as a former New York cab driver, takes a truck-driving job purely for self-gain, but, courtesy of sweet lady-in-distress Laraine Day, he winds up the film in a burst of selfless heroism, leading trucks and Chinese guerrillas in an attack on the Japanese after hearing of their attack on Pearl Harbor.

This was a typical, but under the circumstances, very timely story of how Americans always come through when the chips are really down.

THE NEW YORK TIMES:

In Hollywood heroics come cheap. A little too cheap, one is inclined to think while watching the up-and-at-'em antics of *A Yank on the Burma Road*. . . . It is strangely irresponsible stuff, irresponsible in making a serious business the background for a preposterous love-triangle which only a script writer could believe. It also is irresponsible in its rather patronizing attitude toward the Chinese. . . . *A Yank on the Burma Road* is glib humbug. It is playing tiddledy-winks with high stakes."

Theodore Strauss

Barry Nelson, Keye Luke (center), Laraine Day and Stuart Crawford.

Barry Nelson, Laraine Day, Stuart Crawford in *A Yank on the Burma Road*, the first movie to deal with the attack on Pearl Harbor.

Lionel Atwill, Jack Benny, Carole Lombard, Maude Eburne in *To Be or Not to Be.*

To Be or Not to Be

United Artists

New York release date, March 6, 1942

Presented by Alexander Korda; produced and directed by Ernst Lubitsch; screenplay by Edwin Justus Mayer; from an original story by Ernst Lubitsch and Melchior Lengyel.

CAST: Carole Lombard, Jack Benny, Robert Stack, Felix Bressart, Lionel Atwill, Stanley Ridges, Sig Rumann, Tom Dugan, Charles Halton, George Lynn, Henry Victor, Maude Eburne, Armand Wright, Erno Verebes, Halliwell Hobbes, Miles Mander,

Ernst Lubitsch produced and directed *To Be or Not to Be,* which was based on his own original story and starred Carole Lombard (in her last screen appearance) and Jack Benny as the leading members of a Polish theatrical troupe caught in Warsaw when the Germans invaded Poland. Since the group had been rehearsing an anti-Nazi play they donned the Nazi uniforms they had worn as costumes and proceeded to sabotage the Nazis from the inside. There were a great many laughs as Lombard and Benny, Lubitsch's "Polish" version of the Lunts, undid the best laid plans of the Germans and kept the Gestapo befuddled.

Lubitsch freely mixed laughs in the context of a melodramatic spy-thriller to alternately amusing and suspenseful effect.

After filming was completed on *To Be or Not to Be,* Carole Lombard was killed in a plane crash while on a bond-selling tour on behalf of the war effort.

THE NEW YORK TIMES:

Perhaps there are plenty of persons who can overlook the locale, who can still laugh at Nazi generals. . . . Those patrons will certainly relish the burlesque bravado of this film. And many more will enjoy the glib surprises and suspense of the plot. But it is hard to imagine how any one can take, without batting an eye, a shattering air raid upon Warsaw right after a sequence of farce or the spectacle of Mr. Benny playing a comedy scene with a Gestapo corpse. Mr. Lubitsch had an odd sense of humor—and a tangled script—when he made this film. . . . Miss Lombard . . . is very beautiful and comically adroit, and the feelings which one might imagine her presence would impose are never sensed. This is indeed a glowing tribute to her glowing personality. But Mr. Benny . . . still gives out too much of Jack Benny, the radio comedian. . . . Too bad a little more taste and a little more unity of mood were not put in this film. As it is, one has the strange feeling that Mr. Lubitsch is a Nero, fiddling while Rome burns.

Bosley Crowther

NEWSWEEK:

For the first ten or fifteen minutes you may have the unhappy feeling that the director, in promising comedy amidst an all-too-realistic re-creation of Warsaw's doom, is going to miss his objective by a mile. He comes pretty close to scoring a bull's-eye, however, once Alexander Korda's production settles down to the actual business at hand—which is nothing more or less than providing a good time at the expense of Nazi myth. . . . Lubitsch distinguishes the film's zanier moments with his customary mastery of sly humor and innuendo, and when the story calls for outright melodrama . . . he is more than equal to the occasion. . . . Carole Lombard has never been better than in this, her screen farewell. Her Maria Tura is an attractive, intelligently humorous characterization that is all too rare on the screen and will be rarer from now on. . . .

Darryl Hickman, Robert Young and Marsha Hunt, M-G-M's version of the typical family in *Joe Smith American.*

Joe Smith, American

MGM

New York release date, April 1, 1942

Directed by Richard Thorpe; screenplay by Allen Rivkin; based on the story by Paul Gallico.

CAST: Robert Young, Marsha Hunt, Harvey Stephens, Darryl Hickman, Jonathan Hale, Noel Madison, Don Costello, Joseph Anthony, William Forrest, Russell Hicks, Mark Daniels, William Tannen.

Without resorting to melodrama, MGM's powerful propaganda piece was a compelling testament to the courage and integrity of an "average" American under not only enemy pressure but torture as well.

Robert Young played Joe Smith, son of immigrants, family man (Marsha Hunt was his wife and Darryl Hickman his son), an aircraft factory worker who possessed details of a new bomb-sight of which enemy agents wanted a blueprint. Joe is kidnapped by the Nazi operatives, but even under torture they

Marsha Hunt comforts her husband, Robert Young.

cannot force him to betray his country. He ultimately escapes and is able to lead the FBI to his captors. Joe's coolth and refusal to talk regardless of personal pain and anguish demonstrated the indestructibility—and ultimate triumph—of the American spirit.

THE NEW YORK TIMES:

In its own simple and unassuming way, *Joe Smith, American* ... does more to underscore the deep and indelible reasons why this country is at war than most of the recent million-dollar epics with all their bravura patriotism. ... The author and director have simply taken one commonplace American and shown, in one tense and sharply cut event when his country's safety was at stake, how it was the little things, the small remembrances of what his life had been, that pulled him through.

Theodore Strauss

TIME:

Joe Smith, American is the man Hollywood forgot while it was busy glamorizing World War I doughboys. An aircraft factory worker, he is one of the 14 to 20 civilians it takes to keep a modern fighting man in the field. His story is just the kind of propaganda the U.S. would like to have Hollywood make more of. Adult, informative and entertaining, it klieg-lights the new warfare at a most important spot: the armament production line. ... Until war hits him, Joe is just another untested American. ... Not a high-powered movie, it is a first-rate die for the new propaganda models which Hollywood is readying for mass production.

Robert Young is briefed on a new bombsight by government engineers.

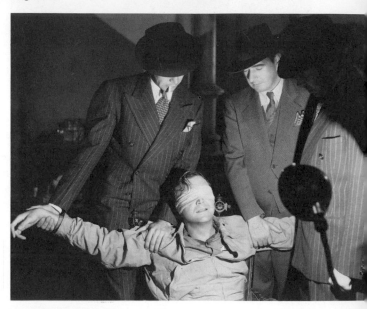
Nazi agents attempt to get information from Robert Young.

Robert Young assists police and FBI in tracking down his Nazi abductors.

Priscilla Lane and Robert Young attempt to convince guests at a social party that they are in fact in the midst of Nazi agents.

Saboteur

Universal Pictures

New York release date, May 7, 1942

Produced by Frank Lloyd; directed by Alfred Hitchcock; screenplay by Peter Viertel, Joan Harrison and Dorothy Parker.

CAST: Priscilla Lane, Robert Cummings, Otto Kruger, Alan Baxter, Clem Bevans, Norman Lloyd, Alma Kruger, Vaughan Glazer, Dorothy Peterson, Ian Wolfe, Frances Carson, Murray Alper, Kathryn Adams.

Alfred Hitchcock's exciting chase melodrama pitted a simple American mechanic against a whole gang of Nazi saboteurs. Robert Cummings, a seemingly unlikely actor for this sort of action-meller, played the hero in the tough spot of being on the run from the law at the same time as he was on the trail of the enemy agents who were responsible for the death of his best friend during an aircraft factory fire they engineered. Cummings had not only to clear his own name of a murder charge but also to prevent further

Robert Cummings and Norman Lloyd in *Saboteur*.

67

Robert Cummings and Priscilla Lane.

sabotage as well. The film, which included a few words about democracy and freedom when the factory worker and traitor confronted each other, was one of Hitchcock's best and wound up with a breath-bating chase which ended fittingly in the torch of the Statue of Liberty in New York harbor.

THE NEW YORK TIMES:

The ardor of Alfred Hitchcock for tales about fifth columnists and spies has already been productive of so many fascinating films that his further commerce with such characters, in this time when they are cluttering up the world, was virtually a social obligation. ... *Saboteur* ... is in the nature of an official report, clearly and keenly appreciative of what is expected from it.

So fast, indeed, is the action and so abundant the breathless events that one might forget, in the hubbub, that there is no logic in this wild-goose chase. There is no reason for the hero undertaking his mad pursuit, since the obvious and sensible method would be to have it conducted by the FBI.

As usual, Mr. Hitchcock and his writers have contrived excuses. But their casual presentation of the FBI as a bunch of bungling dolts, their general disregard of authorized agents and their slur on the Navy Yard police somewhat vitiates the patriotic implications which they have tried to emphasize in the film. One gathers that the nation's safety depends entirely on civilian amateurs.

Bosley Crowther

TIME:

Saboteur is one hour and 45 minutes of almost simonpure melodrama from the hand of the master: Hitchcock. ... Hitchcock, who admits to a liking for murder amid babbling brooks, steps up the excitement of his picture by deftly understating his saboteurs' characters. ... These artful touches serve another purpose which is only incidental to *Saboteur's* melodramatic intent. They warn Americans, as Hollywood has so far failed to do, that fifth columnists can be outwardly clean and patriotic citizens.

Robert Cummings in the clutches of Nazi agents. Norman Lloyd, (left).

James Cagney in *Yankee Doodle Dandy*. Elements of the plot used World War I as a propaganda device to build nationalistic feelings.

Yankee Doodle Dandy

Warner Bros.

New York release date, May 31, 1942

Produced by Jack L. Warner; directed by Michael Curtiz; screenplay by Robert Buckner and Edmund Joseph, based on the story by Robert Buckner.

CAST: James Cagney, Joan Leslie, Walter Huston, Richard Whorf, Irene Manning, George Tobias, Rosemary DeCamp, Jeanne Cagney, Frances Langford, George Barbier, S. Z. Sakall, Walter Catlett, Douglas Croft, Eddie Foy, Jr. Minor Watson, Chester Clute, Odette Myrtil, Patsy Lee Parsons, Capt. Jack Young.

This gigantic hit wartime musical starred James Cagney in the title role of George M. Cohan, patriot and showman supreme. It was a timely film biography of one of America's all-time great flag-wavers, and Cagney's bravura performance won him a well-deserved Oscar. *Yankee Doodle Dandy* combined the rags-to-riches success story of the theatrical Cohan family with exciting and heart-stirring musical nostalgia, highlighting such songs of World War I as "Over There" and "Yankee Doodle Dandy" and celebrating both the life of George M. Cohan and the

James Cagney calls on FDR at the White House in *Yankee Doodle Dandy*.

Richard Whorf, as Sam Harris, Cohan's partner, with James Cagney and Joan Leslie.

American way of life. Movie-goers joined the celebration to the tune of a gross in excess of $5 million.

The film was the last picture Cagney made for Warner Bros. With it his contract was fulfilled and he left Warners to form his own production company and release his films through United Artists.

TIME:

The picture goes overboard with an elaborate presentation of "You're a Grand Old Flag." But the simple re-staging of Cohan's conception of his cocky war song, "Over There," is enough to send movie audiences straight off to battle. . . .

NEW YORK JOURNAL-AMERICAN:

. . . It's unquestionably Mr. Cagney's most brilliant bit of make-believe. He gets over the characterization by suggestion rather than by out-and-out imitation, and a typical gesture here, a well-remembered mannerism there, and, at all times, a buoyant vitality, and it's a performance that has both authority and charm.

Rose Pelswick

NEW YORK POST:

Two wonderful performances keep the picture boiling. Walter Huston makes a marvelous elder Cohan. But front and center is James Cagney whose personal dynamism is a letter-perfect conception of the George M. Cohan the public has known. The gestures and the dances ring the bell of recognition at salient points. But it is the inner spirit that captures the imagination.

Archer Winsten

James Cagney as George M. Cohan. From right to left, his mother, Rosemary DeCamp, his father, Walter Huston, his wife, Joan Leslie, his sister, portrayed by real-life sister Jean Cagney, in the grand finale of "You're a Grand Old Flag."

The Minivers: Walter Pidgeon, Greer Garson, Richard Ney, Clare Sanders, Christopher Severn entertain Teresa Wright.

Mrs. Miniver

MGM

New York release date, June 4, 1942

Produced by Sidney Franklin; directed by William Wyler; screenplay by Arthur Wimperis, George Froeschel, James Hilton and Claudine West; based on the book by Jan Struther.

CAST: Greer Garson, Walter Pidgeon, Teresa Wright, Dame May Whitty, Reginald Owen, Henry Travers, Richard Ney, Henry Wilcoxon, Christopher Severn, Brenda Forbes, Clare Sandars, Marie De Becker, Helmut Dantine, John Abbott, Connie Leon, Rhys Williams.

With its moving and gripping story about the suffering and courage of British civilians in war, *Mrs. Miniver* was an extremely important film. It had tremendous effect on American public opinion and was considered to be of great value in increasing the empathy of Americans for their beleaguered English cousins. One wonders too, in retrospect, whether the film might also have had the dual purpose of sub-liminally preparing Americans for what they might expect if the bombs began to fall at home. *Mrs. Miniver* portrayed the quiet heroism of entire families, of housewives, stationmasters, shopkeepers, of middle-class and of manor-born.

The film centered around the middle-class Miniver family: Greer Garson and Walter Pidgeon, the parents; Richard Ney, Christopher Severn, Clare Sandars, their children. We saw how this family faced the impact of war and also how the war affected the lady in the manor, played by Dame May Whitty, with Teresa Wright her daughter, who loves and marries the oldest Miniver boy, a member of the RAF.

There were many notable scenes in the film: the evacuation of Dunkerque, a harrowing night in a bomb shelter, an intense encounter between Mrs. Miniver and a downed German flyer she captures, a flower show where the community comes together, and countless small moments made memorable by

Greer Garson, Walter Pidgeon and children in *Mrs. Miniver,* the ultimate World War II propaganda movie.

William Wyer's skillful and sensitive direction.

The picture received five Academy Awards: Best Picture, Best Direction, Best Actress (Garson), Best Supporting Actress (Wright) and Best Screenplay. Dore Schary, one of Metro's key production executives at the time, points out that *Mrs. Miniver* "was a portrait of the stereotype Americans had about the English, and that accounted for the film's enormous success. All those stereotypes, of course, had some truth in them because we do know that the English spirit in those days was just extraordinary and it made us feel something very deep and very moving and we responded to it."

There was an ironic note in Greer Garson's winning the Best Actress Oscar for *Mrs. Miniver:* She had accepted the role reluctantly, having been badgered into it by MGM head Louis B. Mayer. Miss Garson objected to playing the mother of a grown

Teresa Wright, Walter Pidgeon, Greer Garson and Richard Ney (whom Garson later married).

son (in fact she later married her screen son, Richard Ney), and Norma Shearer had turned down the role for the same reason when Mayer had initially offered it to her.

THE NEW YORK TIMES:

This is not a war film about soldiers in uniform. This is a film about the people in a small, unpretentious English town on whom the war creeps up slowly, disturbing their tranquil ways of life, then suddenly bursts in devastating fury as the bombs rain down and the Battle of Britain is on. This is a film of modern warfare in which civilians become the frontline fighters and the ingrained courage of the people becomes the nation's most vital strength. This is a film in which a flower show is as pregnant of national spirit as Dunkerque.

... It tells most eloquently of the humor and courage of these people under fire. And the climax is a shattering revelation that it is they, as well as the soldiers, who fight this war.

Two years ago yesterday Winston Churchill gave his memorable address: "We shall go on to the end. ... We shall never surrender." It was most propitious that *Mrs. Miniver* should open on that anniversary. One seeing it can understand why there was no doubt in Mr. Churchill's mind.

Bosley Crowther

TIME:

Mrs. Miniver is that almost impossible feat, a great war picture that photographs the inner meaning, instead of the outward realism of World War II. ... By sensitive understanding and more good humor than most Hollywood comedies achieve, Director

Walter Pidgeon and Greer Garson in their bomb shelter.

Wyler, with reticence, good taste, and an understanding of events ... reflects the war's global havoc without ever taking his cameras off the Minivers' quiet corner of England.

NEW YORK HERALD TRIBUNE:

This is a very fine motion picture as well as a splendid re-affirmation of the things for which the United Nations are fighting. ... The acting is nothing short of inspired. Greer Garson plays the title role with such beauty and dignity that it becomes one of the distinguished performances of this or any other picture. Mr. Pidgeon gives a stalwart and restrained characterization of Mr. Miniver and the romance is handled superlatively by Teresa Wright and Mr. Ney.

... A stirring celebration of the people's part in a people's war. It is a film which you will not forget for a long time after you have seen it. A few works of art succeed in impinging on a time of crisis with stunning force and meaning. *Mrs. Miniver* is one of these."

Howard Barnes

Teresa Wright and Dame May Whitty.

Conrad Veidt and Ann Ayars.

Nazi Agent

MGM

New York release date, June 14, 1942

Produced by Irving Asher; directed by Jules Dassin; screenplay by Paul Gangelin and John Meehan, Jr.; based on an idea by Lother Mendes.

CAST: Conrad Veidt, Ann Ayars, Frank Reicher, Dorothy Tree, Ivan Simpson, William Tannen, Martin Kosleck, Marc Lawrence, Sidney Blackmer, Moroni Olsen.

Nazi Agent made a timely point about national allegiance being stronger than blood relationships.

Conrad Veidt played a dual role in this spy melodrama. He portrayed both a loyal German-born American and his twin, a Nazi official who forces his look-alike sibling into aiding a group of German spies. Veidt goes along at first but kills his evil brother when he gets a chance and then impersonates him in order to get the goods on the spies and find out the extent of their operation. The film built up suspense as one watched Veidt slowly give himself away to the spies even as he learned their secrets.

Jules Dassin made his motion picture directorial

Conrad Veidt played a dual role in *Nazi Agent*.

debut with *Nazi Agent,* which was one of the very successful films produced under Dore Schary's aegis as head of production for MGM's "B" unit.

THE NEW YORK TIMES:

It's an old device but a good one—the substitution of identical twins—which Metro has used as the main twist in *Nazi Agent.* . . . And it makes for a tautly intriguing and sometimes hair-raising spy film such as one can find adequately valid in this day when spies are known to be smooth boys. . . . The film [has] a quiet distinction which has become familiar of late in Metro's "B's." *Nazi Agent* has a lot more to it than some costlier thrill-builders in this line.

Bosley Crowther

Martin Kosleck, character agent who played many Nazi parts in 40s movies, with Conrad Veidt.

Wake Island

Paramount

New York release date, September 1, 1942

Produced by Joseph Sistrom; directed by John Farrow; screenplay by W. R. Burnett and Frank Butler, from the records of the United States Marine Corps.

CAST: Brian Donlevy, Robert Preston, Macdonald Carey, Albert Dekker, William Bendix, Walter Abel, Mikhail Rasumny, Bill Goodwin, Barbara Britton, Damian O'Flynn.

Few films of the period roused the emotions as did *Wake Island,* a stirring, albeit fictionalized, account of the heroic to-the-last-man defense of the Pacific island base, recreated for cinema's sake on the shore of California's Salton Sea. The film succeeded both as wartime propaganda and engrossing entertainment. The story of the sacrifices of the gallant and doomed defenders—movingly portrayed by Brian Donlevy, Robert Preston, Macdonald Carey, William Bendix and others—was nothing less than a clarion call for the defense of freedom and a rallying point for all Americans determined to "remember Wake Island" along with Pearl Harbor. The battle scenes were chillingly realistic.

The film was an enormous hit, as were many of the fact-based fiction films about American fighting men. The numerous excellent documentaries about the war were not popular with civilian audiences, as

Macdonald Carey, Robert Preston, Brian Donlevy in *Wake Island,* the first major motion picture about Americans at war.

Macdonald Carey and Brian Donlevy in *Wake Island,* hailed as a realistic portrayal of our fighting men in World War II.

Dore Schary interestingly notes: "Oddly enough, the documentaries, which were made available to exhibitors for free, were not popular; the exhibitors would offer them but the public would not go to see them. Now they *would* go the next day to a picture with Errol Flynn in which he killed 87 million Germans, because fiction was more interesting, even though it was pertinent to the war, and these pictures always said the right things: 'Nazism must die; never again must we be faced with this horror' and so on. They always said the right things but they were still fiction. If you tried to show *The True Glory* or any of the Army or Navy documentaries, the public didn't want to see them because that was for real, those were real names and real people dying."

THE NEW YORK TIMES:

Here is a film which should surely bring a surge of pride to every patriot's breast. And here is a film for which its makers deserve a sincere salute. Except for the use of fictional names and a very slight contrivance of plot, it might be a literal document of the manner in which the Wake detachment of Marines fought and died in the finest tradition of their tough and indomitable corps. A realistic picture about heroes who do not pose as such . . . with never a big theatrical gesture or a comment that doesn't ring true.

William Bendix arrives for a new assignment.

William Bendix and Robert Preston will snag the plaudits for their performances as tough Marines. A more respectable pair of Leathernecks has not come along since Flagg and Quirt.

This reviewer first saw *Wake Island* at the Quantico Marine base last week. On that occasion, some 2,000 fighters cheered it with thunderous applause. Those Marines have a personal interest involved. We will confidently stand on their response.

Bosley Crowther

NEW YORK HERALD TRIBUNE:

The acting is as close to perfect as one could possibly ask, even in an epic of this stature. Brian Donlevy is utterly right as the commanding major. Robert Preston and William Bendix contribute an undercurrent of captivating comedy as a couple of tough Marine pals. Macdonald Carey's portrait of a grief-stricken, vengeful flyer is entirely convincing, and Albert Dekker, Walter Abel and the others give inspired performances. John Farrow's staging matches the material and the portrayals. *Wake Island* is a memorable motion picture.

Howard Barnes

NEWSWEEK:

Although the United States has been at war for nine months, *Wake Island* is Hollywood's first intelligent, honest, and completely successful attempt to dramatize the deeds of an American force on a fighting front.

Martin Kosleck questions Dana Andrews in *Berlin Correspondent*.

Berlin Correspondent

20th Century-Fox

New York release date, September 3, 1942

Produced by Bryan Foy; directed by Eugene Forde; screenplay by Steve Fisher and Jack Andrews.

CAST: Virginia Gilmore, Dana Andrews, Mona Maris, Martin Kosleck, Sig Rumann, Kurt Katch, Erwin Kalser, Torben Meyer, William Edmunds, Hans Schumm, Leonard Mudie, Hans von Morhart, Curt Furberg, Henry Rowland, Christian Rub.

This was a brash melodrama about an American war correspondent who attempts to steal Axis military secrets in Berlin and rescue his informant from the Gestapo—all before the surprise attack on Pearl Harbor. The film seemed to be a cheap copy of "Mister V," a British picture which had Leslie Howard involved in similar exploits, but much more effectively and with hilariously satirical moments at German expense. The American effort mixed several un-

Sig Rumann, who also played a number of Nazi types during the war years, with Dana Andrews posing as a Nazi.

successful attempts to satirize the Germans among its farfetched plot devices, but all to little purpose.

future existence to be trifled with in cheap melodramas like *Berlin Correspondent*.

Thomas M. Pryor

THE NEW YORK TIMES:

Berlin Correspondent is the type of picture that is known in the trade as a program filler. . . . For what the United Nations are fighting to stamp out in Germany today is too terribly real and vital to our

NEW YORK HERALD TRIBUNE:

More than a few of the best sequences of *Berlin Correspondent* lose weight soon after the synthetic suspense has worn off, when one has time to appreciate how implausible they actually are.

Sig Rumann and Dana Andrews.

Dana Andrews and Sig Rumann.

Across the Pacific

Warner Bros.

New York, release date, September 4, 1942

Produced by Jerry Wald; directed by John Huston; screenplay by Richard Macauley; based on a story by Robert Carson.

CAST: Humphrey Bogart, Mary Astor, Sydney Greenstreet, Charles Halton, Sen Yung, Roland Got, Lee Tung Foo, Frank Wilcox, Paul Stanton, Lester Matthews, John Hamilton, Tom Stevenson, Roland Drew, Monte Blue, Chester Gan, Richard Loo, Keye Luke, Kam Tong, Spencer Chan, Rudy Robles.

Director John Huston's third film dealt, as had his first, *The Maltese Falcon,* with international intrigue. This time he had Humphrey Bogart embroiled in an espionage-counter-espionage thriller about Japanese agents in Panama just before Pearl Harbor. There were some old familiar bits in the script, which presented Bogart as an army officer pretending to be a traitor in order to trap the enemy operatives. It also had Mary Astor as "the girl," on her way to Panama to find out what became of her planter-father, who naturally had gotten involved in the evil work of the treacherous Japanese. Although Bogart took the customary terrific beating before routing the enemy, he

Humphrey Bogart in *Across the Pacific,* directed by John Huston and teaming Bogart with Mary Astor and Sydney Greenstreet.

did wind up foiling their nefarious scheme for shutting down the canal—and, of course, he won Miss Astor too.

NEW YORK HERALD TRIBUNE:

Honors are about even when it comes to the staging and the acting. John Huston . . . has directed the film with the subtle blood-and-thunder accents that . . . Hitchcock has established as the criteria of true screen melodrama.

Bogart is triumphant. . . . Greenstreet justifies all the promise he showed in *The Maltese Falcon*. And Mary Astor is better than she has been in a long list of assignments.

W.H.

THE NEW YORK TIMES:

This time it is certain: Alfred Hitchcock, Carol Reed and all other directors who have hit the top flight with melodramas will have to make space for John Huston. For young Mr. Huston, who cracked out a scorching thriller in *The Maltese Falcon* last year, has done it again in *Across the Pacific* . . . a spy picture this time which tingles with fearful uncertainties and glints with the sheen of blue steel."

Bosley Crowther

Humphrey Bogart and Mary Astor.

Humphrey Bogart.

For Me and My Gal

MGM

New York release date, October 21, 1942

Produced by Arthur Freed; directed by Busby Berkeley; screenplay by Richard Sherman, Fred Finklehoffe and Sid Silvers; original story by Howard Emmett Rogers; song "For Me and My Gal" by George W. Meyer, Edgar Leslie and E. Ray Goetz.

CAST: Judy Garland, George Murphy, Gene Kelly, Marta Eggerth, Ben Blue, Horace (Stephen) McNally, Richard Quine, Lucille Norman, Keenan Wynn.

MGM used a World War I and vaudeville theme to make this patriotic film for release late in 1942. There were many musicals released during the war years with plots about soldiers and girls. This· one stands out because of a very startling scene in which Gene Kelly slams a trunk lid down on his hand to wound himself in order to be draft exempt. Although this element of the plot is later resolved and Judy

Gene Kelly looks on with special feeling as Judy Garland entertains the troops in *For Me and My Gal*.

George Murphy, Judy Garland and Gene Kelly on stage.

Garland and Kelly eventually unite, the idea of putting personal wishes over duty to country really had an impact on audiences of the day.

NEW YORK HERALD TRIBUNE:

. . . It has more than one moment of effective entertainment. With the original World War tied into the climax, it has a particular dramatic and emotional punch at the moment. . . . There are some moving interludes showing the impact of war on individualists and the manner in which the amusement profession rose to the occasion 25 years ago exactly as it has today.

Howard Barnes

THE NEW YORK TIMES:

. . . Mr. Kelly, who has a dancer's talents, has been pressed a bit too far in his first film role. He has been forced to act brassy like Pal Joey during the early part of the film and then turn about and play a modest imitation of Sergeant York at the end."

Bosley Crowther

Ben Blue, George Murphy, Gene Kelly and Judy Garland.

Fay Bainter played Mrs. Hadley, a society woman inconvenienced by the war.

The War Against Mrs. Hadley

MGM

New York release date, November 25, 1942

Produced by Irving Asher; directed by Harold S. Bucquet, screenplay by George Oppenheimer.

CAST: Edward Arnold, Fay Bainter, Richard Ney, Jean Rogers, Sara Allgood, Spring Byington, Van Johnson, Isobel Elsom, Frances Rafferty, Dorothy Morris, Halliwell Hobbes, Connie Gilchrist, Horace McNally, Miles Mander, "Rags" Ragland, Mark Daniels, Carl Switzer.

The War Against Mrs. Hadley was a particularly pertinent film dealing with civilian homefront adjustments to the war. Its story centered on a Washington, D.C., society matron, Fay Bainter, who tried to keep her secure and placid life from being disrupted by the demands placed upon it by the national war effort. The filmmakers drew a fine portrait of an overprotected American woman who thought she could avoid the grimmer realities of everyone else's lives and keep the shadow of the world conflict from her door. By fade-out time, of course, Mrs. Hadley—

with a little help from her son, Richard Ney, daughter, Jean Rogers, and friends—has seen the error of her ways and realized that the survival of her own way of life cannot be separated from the defense of democracy itself.

This was another of the films made at MGM by Dore Schary's unit. Schary comments: "This was a film that did very well and hit right at the isolationist group. We belted away at that."

NEW YORK HERALD TRIBUNE:

Although there is never any doubt that Mrs. Hadley will lose her little war against the United States, the chances are that you will enjoy the proceedings. Mrs. Hadley is finally overwhelmed by democracy, and a good thing, too.

Joseph Pihodna

THE NEW YORK TIMES:

With the very best of intentions, but with little dramatic artistry, Metro has tried to make a picture to

Miles Mander, Fay Bainter, and
Spring Byington.

point the stern moral that complacency and self-interest are futile in America at war. [The film] should have come sooner, if at all. For the simple fact is that Mrs. Hadley, the principal character in this tale, is not only an inordinate person, barely reflective of an average American type, but even her sort is as dated as a last winter's coffee can.

It really does little more than confute, with its snobbish devices, the essential spirit of true democracy. If this film is, as some have hailed it, the American *Mrs. Miniver,* then a lot of us must have grave illusions about our own (or the English) way of life.

Bosley Crowther

Edward Arnold, Jean Rogers, Miles Mander, Fay Bainter, Richard Ney, Spring Byington in *The War Against Mrs. Hadley.*

Humphrey Bogart in front of his Casablanca café.

Casablanca

Warner Bros.

New York release date, November 26, 1942

Produced by Hal B. Wallis; directed by Michael Curtiz; screenplay by Julius J. and Philip G. Epstein and Howard Koch; from a play by Murray Burnett and Joan Alison.

CAST: Humphrey Bogart, Ingrid Bergman, Paul Henreid, Claude Rains, Conrad Veidt, Sydney Greenstreet, Peter Lorre, S. Z. Sakall, Madeleine LeBeau, Dooley Wilson, Joy Page, John Qualen, Leonid Kinskey, Helmut Dantine, Curt Bois, Marcel Dalio, Corinna Mura, Ludwig Stossel, Ilka Gruning, Charles La Torre, Frank Puglia, Dan Seymour.

With the Allied invasion of North Africa underway when *Casablanca* was released, it was an extremely topical film. (Warners had, in fact, advanced the release date from January to November when the news of the Allied Expeditionary Force landing was received. The company also rushed a print to Africa for viewing by the troops). With what seemed prophetic insight, the movie exposed the intrigue, political maneuvering and anti-fascist resentments which many felt must have been the background for the Allied offensive.

Humphrey Bogart reached a peak in his career

Paul Henreid, Ingrid Bergman, Claude Rains and Humphrey Bogart in the classic *Casablanca*.

Humphrey Bogart and Ingrid Bergman, an unlikely but fascinating duo.

with the role of cynical Café Americain-owner Rick, a neutral, disillusioned democrat interested only in self-survival—until he re-encountered his ex-lover Ingrid Bergan, who was fleeing the Nazis with her husband, underground resistance leader Paul Henreid.

Against the background of a city teeming with the displaced and disassociated humanity war creates, Bogart's inner conflicts were played out as he was inevitably drawn into the struggle, assisting Bergman and Henreid in their flight.

Involved in director Michael Curtiz's measured swirl of intrigue and suspense were Sydney Greenstreet, as a black-marketeer; Peter Lorre, as a dealer in anything extra-legal; Conrad Veidt, as a determined Nazi officer; Claude Rains, as a Vichy police official; and Dooley Wilson, as Sam, the café's pianist and Rick's only trusted friend.

Casablanca received Academy Awards for Best Picture, Best Director and Best Screenplay. It has become a keystone film of the Bogart cult and a landmark film in the history of screen entertainment.

THE NEW YORK TIMES:

. . . A picture which makes the spine tingle and the heart take a leap. They have turned the incisive trick of draping a tender love story within the folds of a tight topical theme. They have used Mr. Bogart's personality . . . to inject a cold point of tough resistance to evil forces afoot in Europe today. And they have so combined sentiment, humor and pathos with taut melodrama and bristling intrigue that the result is a highly entertaining and even inspiring film. . . . One of the year's most exciting and trenchant films. It certainly won't make Vichy happy—but that's just another point for it.

Bosley Crowther

Claude Rains, one of the great character actors of all time, supported Humphrey Bogart in *Casablanca*.

NEW YORK HERALD TRIBUNE:

... Humphrey Bogart and Sydney Greenstreet ... give the production ominous and violent potentialities. Meanwhile, there is Ingrid Bergman, playing the heroine of a war picture with all her appealing authority and beauty. ... *Casablanca* has a continuity which is a clever blend of melodrama and meaning. ... The show makes a great deal of sense, in addition to being a striking thriller. It has sustained interest as well as excitement.

Howard Barnes

NEWSWEEK:

Although the resulting melodrama is top-heavy with plot and subplot ... only the most critical will take time out to carp. *Casablanca*—even more so, now that its theme has lost its poignant immediacy—is absorbing escapist entertainment. For one thing, Michael Curtiz is able to fall back on atmosphere when suspense lags. For another, far less interesting material would seem exciting with the top-notch performances turned in by the stars and a surprisingly strong cast.

Bergman and Bogie.

TIME:

Before the U.S. seizure of Morocco handed Warner Bros. some of the most dazzling promotion in years, *Casablanca* was just an exotic location for a topical melodrama. This picture is about some refugees who were stranded in Casablanca and some of the people who helped or hindered them. ... Bogart, so tough that at one moment he looks like Buster Keaton playing Paul Gauguin. ... Nothing short of an invasion could add much to *Casablanca*.

Humphrey Bogart with Dooley Wilson, who introduced the song "As Time Goes By."

The great finale of *Casablanca* with Claude Rains, Paul Henreid, Humphrey Bogart and Ingrid Bergman.

Robert Young with Margaret O'Brien in *Journey for Margaret,* the film that launched Margaret as the foremost child star of the 40s.

Journey for Margaret

MGM

New York release date, December 17, 1942

Produced by B. P. Fineman; directed by Major W. S. Van Dyke; screenplay by David Hertz and William Ludwig; based on the book by William L. White.

CAST: Robert Young, Laraine Day, Fay Bainter, Nigel Bruce, Margaret O'Brien, William Severn, Elisabeth Risdon, Doris Lloyd, Halliwell Hobbes, Heather Thatcher, Jill Esmond, G. P. Huntley, Jr., Lisa Golm.

While on assignment in Britain, American correspondent William L. White adopted and brought back to the United States a little war orphan about whom he subsequently wrote a best-selling book, *A Journey for Margaret,* which became the basis for the movie.

Tiny five-year-old Margaret O'Brien captured the hearts of American moviegoers and became the biggest child star since Shirley Temple with her performance as Margaret White, the orphan of the Blitz adopted by screen newspaperman John Davis (Robert Young).

The story recounted how, after an air raid, Davis,

Robert Young holding William Severn,
Laraine Day holding Margaret O'Brien.

angered over the destruction he has witnessed and embittered by the injury of his wife and the loss of their unborn child, visited a center for homeless children, where he encountered Margaret and a little boy, Peter. The reporter and his wife become fond of the children and eventually adopt them and bring them to America and safety.

A Journey for Margaret was a tremendous hit, and a touching and moving story about Hitler's most innocent victims.

THE NEW YORK TIMES:

When the big bombers come, little children do not count for much. . . . What can happen to childhood in that horror is the substance of one of the year's rare and shining achievements from Hollywood. [It is] a picture of tortured childhood that will not soon be forgotten by any one who has ever loved a child. For once, Hollywood has given us something to be grateful for. . . . Of little Margaret O'Brien, herself a wartime migrant, who plays the title role, one can hardly say that she gives a performance—it is too taut and true for that. The children are so moving that one is almost apt to overlook the really fine performance of Robert Young in one of the most unpretentious and sensitive portraits he has given.

There is a hurt in *Journey for Margaret,* a hurt that will remain long after these desperate years and until these children have learned again to trust the sky—and more, to trust human beings. It is going to

90

Robert Young and Margaret O'Brien.

take more than victory alone to dry these tears. But the compassion that marks *Journey for Margaret* will go far to help them."

Theodore Strauss

NEW YORK HERALD TRIBUNE:

Robert Young does an excellent restrained acting job as John Davis, the American correspondent who, on assignment, interviews the head of a home for bombed and shell-shocked children of all ages.

Journey for Margaret is an uncomplicated exposition of the rather complex problem facing children in modern warfare. The film's most touching scenes . . . are those showing how the youngsters react to the war.

Joseph Pihodna

Robert Young and Margaret O'Brien.

Ronald Colman and Greer Garson in *Random Harvest,* another movie about World War I to build patriotism and home-front morale.

Random Harvest

MGM

New York release date, December 17, 1942

Produced by Sidney Franklin; directed by Mervyn LeRoy; screenplay by Claudine West, George Froeschel and Arthur Wimperis; based on the novel by James Hilton.

CAST: Ronald Colman, Greer Garson, Philip Dorn, Susan Peters, Henry Travers, Reginald Owen, Bramwell Fletcher, Rhys Williams, Una O'Connor, Charles Waldron, Elizabeth Risdon, Melville Cooper, Margaret Wycherly, Aubrey Mather, Arthur Margetson, Alan Napier, Jill Esmond, Marta Linden, Ann Richards, Norma Varden, David Cavendish, Ivan Simpson, Marie de Becker.

A tale of a shell-shocked World War I veteran suffering from amnesia, *Random Harvest* was a romantic soft-focus drama whose underlying theme of the effects of war on a single man was wrapped in a touching love story.

Ronald Colman played the amnesiac soldier who meets a beautiful dancer, Greer Garson, on Armistice Day, falls in love and marries her. They settle down in a little cottage and live happily for three years until one day when he is away from home and is struck by a cab. The accident causes him to regain his lost memory and return to the home and wealthy position he had left before the war. The remainder of the film deals with Miss Garson's attempts to find him and, when she does, how she goes about rekindling his memory of their romance and marriage.

Based on James Hilton's best-selling novel, *Random Harvest* was a huge hit and a moving, albeit sentimental, motion picture.

THE NEW YORK TIMES:

... For all its emotional excess, *Random Harvest* is a strangely empty film. Its characters are creatures of fortune, not partisans in determining their own fates ... they never seem real. ...

Bosley Crowther

NEW YORK HERALD TRIBUNE:

... The leading roles are played with power and feeling by Ronald Colman and Greer Garson. With more rigid adaptation and cutting, it might have stood up artistically as strongly as it promises to do at the box office. ... As it is, the players contribute far more to *Random Harvest* than the other craftsmen who worked on it. ... The valid suspense of a highly contrived situation ebbs after more than two hours of rather pedestrian exposition. The subject matter and treatment are definitely unworthy of the acting.

Colman has never been more stoically appealing. ... Miss Garson is radiantly persuasive as the girl from the music halls who marries him twice. ... Novels should be handled astringently on the screen. This one betrays its literary origins in the worst way. ...

Howard Barnes

TIME:

Random Harvest is a first-rate film made from James Hilton's second-rate novel of the same name. It is distinguished by 1) a moving love story, 2) the unveiling of Miss Garson's interesting legs. ...

Ronald Colman and Greer Garson in *Random Harvest*, the movie that exposed her legs.

Ronald Colman and his film family.

John Mills.

In Which We Serve

United Artists

New York release date, December 23, 1942

Produced, written and scored by Noël Coward; directed by Mr. Coward and David Lean.

CAST: Noël Coward, Bernard Miles, John Mills, Celia Johnson, Kay Walsh, Joyce Carey, Derek Elphinstone, Robert Sansom, Philip Friend, Michael Wilding, Hubert Gregg, Ballard Berkeley, James Donald, Kenneth Carton, Walter Fitzgerald, Gerald Case, Ann Stephens, Daniel Massey, Dora Gregory, Kathleen Harrison, George Carney, Richard Attenborough.

In Which We Serve, a British film, was a remarkable tribute not only to the spirit of the western democracies but also to the spirit of embattled humanity wherever men fought for freedom's sake.

Essentially the film was a biography of a ship, the British destroyer *Torrin,* from the time of her launching to her sinking by the Germans in the Mediterranean. It was also the epic story of the men who

served on her, and author-director Noël Coward brought their personal lives into sharp and compelling focus as the background for their heroism.

Coward, who co-directed the film with David Lean, starred as the *Torrin's* captain. *In Which We Serve* was made with the official collaboration of the Royal Navy and the Ministry of Information and was a stirring contribution to the war effort, unsurpassed in its summing up of the Allied cause.

Before its U.S. exhibition, *In Which We Serve* ran afoul of the old-maidish Hays office, Hollywood's official censor, which felt that some of the words uttered by the *Torrin's* crew during moments of stress were too strong for American audiences—even though such persons as King George VI, Queen Elizabeth, Winston Churchill and Mrs. Franklin D. Roosevelt had heard them without noticeable distress—and demanded the excision of "God," "hell," "damn," and "bastard" from the soundtrack. This created in England a furor which went all the way into the House

John Mills in *In Which We Serve*, written and produced by Noël Coward.

of Commons. Ultimately the Hays office assented to everything but "bastard." In Britain, the censors had even allowed the retention of the objectionable (to the English) expletive "bloody," which was perfectly acceptable stateside.

THE NEW YORK TIMES:
There have been other pictures which have vividly and movingly conveyed in terms of human emotion the cruel realities of this present war. None has yet done it so sharply and so truly as *In Which We Serve*.

"This is the story of a ship," says the voice of Mr. Coward to introduce the opening sequence of the picture. . . . But it is more . . . it is the story of man's heroic soul and the selfless, indomitable spirit by which a whole nation endures.

Celia Johnson.

Noël Coward in *In Which We Serve*. He also co-directed the film with David Lean.

John Mills and Kay Walsh.

For the great thing which Mr. Coward has accomplished in this film is a full and complete expression of national fortitude.

. . . This devotion of men to their ship and to their mates is a subtle symbolization of everything that they are. The ship represents themselves, their families. It is their nation. It is their world.

Mr. Coward has written and he and David Lean directed this film out of knowledge and deep compassion for the people and the subject of which they treat.

We may yet see a picture more rational about the large implications of this war. But this observer does not expect ever to see anything more moving. . . .

Bosley Crowther

NEW YORK HERALD TRIBUNE:

There have been rumors that a truly great motion picture was coming to New York. They were triumphantly confirmed at the Capitol. [*In Which We Serve*] looms majestically over all the pictures and plays which have sought to give definition and emotional meaning to the present conflict. Beyond that, it is a masterpiece of film making.

Not at any time, has there been a reconstruction of human experience in the making which could touch the savage grandeur and compassion of this production. It has heart, beauty and eternal verity. *In Which We Serve* is far more than a magnificent war film. It is a stirring testament to men of good will, in whatever age they may have loved, fought and endured.

. . . Coward . . . has immediately commanded an extremely elusive art form. There is a penultimate scene, for example, in which the *Torrin's* captain bids

Men escaping their sinking destroyer.

The *Torrin's* captain, Noël Coward, comforts a wounded crewman, Richard Attenborough.

farewell to the remnants of his crew on an Alexandria dock, which is as powerful and moving a climax to a film as I have ever seen.

Howard Barnes

NEWSWEEK:

... The finest film to come out of the war.... One of the screen's proudest achievements at any time and in any country.... Both dramatically and emotionally, this is a screen experience that is as unusual as it is different from anything Coward has ever contrived before for stage or screen.

Men hang on to lifeboat after their destroyer has been sunk. Noël Coward and John Mills are at extreme right.

Lucky Jordan

Paramount

New York release date, January 24, 1943

Produced by Fred Kohlmar; directed by Frank Tuttle; screenplay by Darrel Ware and Karl Tunberg; based on a story by Charles Leonard.

CAST: Alan Ladd, Helen Walker, Marie McDonald, Mabel Paige, Sheldon Leonard, Lloyd Corrigan, Russell Hoyt, Joan Wengraf, Dave Willock.

When you've got a hot new box-office star—in this case Alan Ladd—who's became a hit in gangster roles, and you want to do your part for the war effort, how do you go about it? What Paramount did was mix up the gangsters with espionage and sabotage and hope for the best, commercially if not artistically. The incredible script presented Ladd in the role of a poolroom racketeer who gets drafted despite his sincere efforts to avoid it. Naturally he's a problem soldier and soon winds up in the guardhouse, only to escape and get involved in an international spy ring. But ultimately he sees "the right path," follows it and ends up saving the day for Mom, Old Glory and Paramount's accountants.

NEW YORK HERALD TRIBUNE:

It's still cops and robbers, no matter how you slice it.... How [Alan Ladd] finally manages to cover himself with glory and gain the good graces of Army officials is a bit hard to swallow.... Mr. Ware and Mr. Tunberg are not above dragging in mother love as the reason the gangster changes from a selfish killer to a patriot.

Joseph Pihodna

TIME:

Lucky Jordan deals with a question that seems to trouble some scenarists: where do U.S. gangsters fit into the war effort?... As a sociological treatise, *Lucky Jordan* shows that U.S. gangsters are infinitely nicer than Nazis because 1) they are Americans, 2) they do not like to "go around beating up old women."

Gig Young (left) and John Ridgely (right) in *Air Force.*

Air Force

Warner Bros.

New York release date, February 3, 1943

Produced by Hal B. Wallis; directed by Howard Hawks; screenplay by Dudley Nichols.

CAST: John Ridgely, Gig Young, Arthur Kennedy, Charles Drake, Harry Carey, George Tobias, Ward Wood, Ray Montgomery, John Garfield, James Brown, Stanley Ridges, Willard Robertson, Moroni Olsen, Edward S. Brophy, Richard Lane, Bill Crago, Faye Emerson, Addison Richards, James Flavin, Ann Doran, Dorothy Peterson.

Made with the full cooperation of the Army Air Corps—and at their suggestion—Howard Hawks' high-flying epic, based on true incidents from Army files, was dedicated to the simple purpose of showing how U.S. airmen fight. It achieved its purpose.

Air Force followed a single Flying Fortress, named *Mary Ann,* and her crew, from take-off at San Francisco on December 6, 1941, to besieged Hickam Field in Hawaii the following morning; then on to the Philippines and subsequently some breath-taking and spectacularly photographed air battles in the South Pacific. Severely damaged, the *Mary Ann* ultimately limped to an Australian beach after valiantly fighting in the battle of the Coral Sea.

For the film, most of which was shot near Tampa, Florida, Hawks was given use of an actual Flying Fortress, although interiors were shot in a $40,000 model. The actual plane was later lost in action in the South Pacific. Audiences got an intimate look at the plane, how it worked, and how the air war was being fought.

Along the way there was the usual mixture of human drama and comic relief which brought the individual crew members (played by John Ridgely, Harry Carey, John Garfield, George Tobias and others) into sharp but never distracting focus. Hawks (himself a veteran of the World War I Air Corps) made his crewmen seem ordinary fighters and thoroughly credible.

John Garfield and Gig Young.

John Garfield.

Air Force was an impressive and engrossing screen achievement.

TIME:

. . . A superbly thrilling show, it is easily the best aviation film to date. Its heroine is a Flying Fortress. . . . The *Mary Ann* and her crew, a composite of many ships and men, fight in every important air battle from Pearl Harbor to the Coral Sea. . . . In this story of one ship, *Air Force* rolls up all the excitement of the air war in the Pacific. . . .

THE NEW YORK TIMES:

. . . Although it draws about the longest and most pliant bow that has ever been drawn in the line of fanciful war films and goes completely overboard in the last reel, it is still a continuously fascinating, frequently thrilling and occasionally exalting show which leaves you limp and triumphant at the end of its two-hour ordeal.

. . . Inspired by the brilliant record which our Army fliers hung up, [Nichols and Hawks] gave way completely to their boundless enthusiasm and awe and ripped out a picture which tingles with the passion of spirits aglow. . . . Mr. Hawks has directed the action for tremendous impact. . . . The air fights, most of which are seen down gun barrels, are thrilling and highly accomplished special effects. . . . Maybe the story is high-flown, maybe it overdraws a recorded fact a bit. We'd hate to think it couldn't happen—or didn't—because it certainly leaves you feeling awfully good.

Bosley Crowther

John Garfield and men in *Air Force,* a wartime epic biography of a plane in the Air Corps.

Thomas Mitchell and Henry Fonda in
Immortal Sergeant.

Immortal Sergeant

20th Century-Fox

New York release date, February 3, 1943

Produced by Lamarr Trotti; directed by John Stahl; screenplay by Mr. Trotti; based on the novel by John Brophy.

CAST: Henry Fonda, Maureen O'Hara, Thomas Mitchell, Allyn Joslyn, Reginald Gardiner, Melville Cooper, Bramwell Fletcher, Morton Lowry, Donald Stuart, Jean Prescott, Heather Wilde.

Immortal Sergeant, essentially an "inspirational" film, told of a battle-toughened non-commissioned officer (Thomas Mitchell) and of his effect on a green corporal under his command. Henry Fonda played the young soldier with quiet resolve, giving credibility to his ultimate character transformation from a timid, insecure civilian-soldier into an effective combat leader. The overall emphasis in the film, however, was more on well-staged desert fighting than on the psy-

chology of its characters, much to the excitement of its audiences.

THE NEW YORK TIMES:

The film's collaborators have tried to dramatize the simple sense of duty that pushes on the man in the ranks when common sense and even military honor would excuse his surrender to the enemy. But, instead of keeping to the point, the authors have spliced their story with flashbacks to a vapid little romance. . . . And they have not been content to let his action stand as his contribution to the success of the greater fight; they have paid him off with the Distinguished Service Cross, a lieutenancy, publicity and, of course, the girl. In short, Corporal Spence reaps a handsome profit—which seems to obscure his more important victory.

Immortal Sergeant might have been a better film

101

Thomas Mitchell and Henry Fonda.

if it had more of the courage it relates. As it is, its truth is half-hearted; its hokum gets the best of it.

Theodore Strauss

TIME:

Hollywood's first picture of the Libyan battlefront, at once makes its audience feel that they have seen it all somewhere before. By the time the first soldier has bit the sand, the film identifies itself: it is none other than Hollywood's old friend, the Foreign Legion of *Beau Geste* vintage, jerked from the shelf and clothed in a new British uniform. . . . A nostalgic, phony tale, *Sergeant* is often exciting, but at its best it looks like the right battle in the wrong war.

Alan Jocelyn, Henry Fonda, Thomas Mitchell in *Immortal Sergeant*, one of the few movies that glorified the infantry.

Kent Smith and Bonita Granville.

Hitler's Children

RKO

New York release date, February 24, 1943

Produced by Edward A. Golden; directed by Edward Dmytryk; screenplay by Emmet Lavery; based on the book *Education for Death* by Gregor Ziemer.

CAST: Kent Smith, Bonita Granville, Tim Holt, Otto Kruger, H. B. Warner, Lloyd Corrigan, Hans Conreid, Erford Gage, Nancy Gates, Gavin Muir.

This Hollywood account of the indoctrination of young Germans with Hitlerian and National Socialist ideals bogged down in sentimentality through its resort to the routine of the old reliable boy-girl plot, wherein Tim Holt is a Nazified youth and Bonita Granville isn't and they love each other despite the fact that she's marked for sterilization because she's deemed unfit to bear illegitimate children for the Führer. Ultimately, of course, she converts Tim to her way of thinking so they can die defiantly together, and what might have been a more hard-hitting treatment of the subversion of young minds gets lost amid romantics and by now familiar Nazi villainry.

Bonita Granville, Tim Holt, Nancy Gates, and Kent Smith in *Hitler's Children.*

Bonita Granville, Otto Kruger, and Hans Conreid.

The film was a sleeper, possibly because it titillated audiences with its quasi-lurid revelations about the Nazi brutalization of young women.

THE NEW YORK TIMES:

The grim and terrifying aspects of the Nazi perversion of German youth—the evils of mass dehumanization by which a blind and brutal war machine was built—have been but narrowly suggested and vaguely realized in RKO's *Hitler's Children*. . . . This fictionized version of Gregor Ziemer's factual *Education for Youth* is an obvious, conventional melodrama set against a background of pre-war Germany . . . old-stuff to those who read the papers and unreflective of the deeper drama involved.

Bosley Crowther

Tim Holt being indoctrinated as a Hitler Youth.

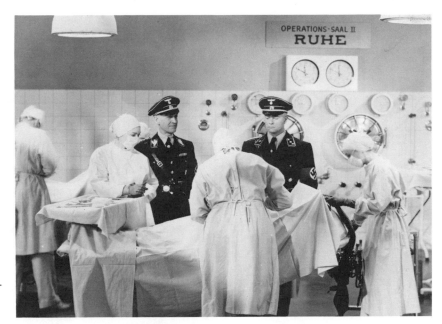

Otto Kruger shows Tim Holt a sterilization operation.

NEW YORK HERALD TRIBUNE:

. . . A curiously compromised production . . . makes its points with brutal emphasis. Both in the treatment and the direction, the picture is more sensational than dramatically effective. . . . The best parts of *Hitler's Children* are very good indeed. Emmet Lavery, who wrote the script, and Edward Dmytryk, who staged it, have chronicled the poisonous propaganda of National Socialism, as it affected German youth, in some striking scenes. They have demonstrated its power over adolescents, in tracing the muted love affair. . . . It is strong anti-Nazi propaganda. It has not been woven into a defined and moving show.

Howard Barnes

Hitler's Children shocked Americans with its depictions of Nazi indoctrination of young people.

Mickey Rooney as the Western Union delivery boy in *The Human Comedy*, with Donna Reed, James Craig, Marsha Hunt, and Van Johnson.

The Human Comedy

MGM

New York release date, March 2, 1943

Produced and directed by Clarence Brown, screenplay by Howard Estabrook, from the story by William Saroyan.

CAST: Mickey Rooney, Frank Morgan, James Craig, Marsha Hunt, Fay Bainter, Ray Collins, Van Johnson, Donna Reed, Jack Jenkins, Dorothy Morris, John Craven, Ann Ayars, Mary Nash, Henry O'Neill, Katharine Alexander, Alan Baxter, David Holt, Darryl Hickman, Barry Nelson, Byron Foulger, Bob Mitchum, Carl "Alfalfa" Switzer, Dcn Defore, Rita Quigley, Clem Bevans, Adeline De Walt Reynolds.

Although *The Human Comedy* received mixed notices it was an important home front morale film. Mickey Rooney gave a touching and believable performance as the young boy in a small town who must face the responsibilities of growing up added to the responsibilities of growing up during a war. As the Western Union delivery boy, it is his undesirable task to deliver telegrams in his small home town during a time when a telegram can only mean that a loved one—a son, a husband—has been killed or wounded in action.

THE NEW YORK TIMES:

. . . Here, cheek by jowl and overlapping, are set some most charming bits of motion-picture expression and some most maudlin gobs of cinematic goo. Here, in an almost formless tribute to the goodness and sweetness of man's soul, are spliced some quick, penetrating glimpses with long stretches of sheer banality. Here, in a picture which endeavors to speak such truths about Americans as should be spoken, pop up such artificialities as make one squirm with rank embarrassment.

Mickey Rooney and unidentified player.

... The whole simple idea of the story is that people are essentially good and that sorrow is a grim, inevitable burden and that faith and love will elevate men's hearts. This is a comforting idea ... and one which has been the basis of fine literature since story-telling began. But when Mr. Saroyan states these ageless and elemental facts by having his characters give out with speeches which sound upon the screen like sermons delivered from pulpits; when Clarence Brown ... backs them up with soulful and tear-jerking music ... then the dignity and simplicity of the ideas shade off into cheap pretentiousness.

"There are a few moments of extraordinary beauty that pop out in the film now and then, such as little Ulysses asking Homer with infinite anxiety in a casual conversation not to leave home....

... The performances are generally excellent, especially that of Mr. Rooney as the sensitive boy ... and the others in the cast are attractive, especially little Jack Jenkins as 4-year-old Ulysses.

Bosley Crowther

TIME:

The Human Comedy is a faithful translation of William Saroyan's novel; hence it is like no other picture that ever came out of Hollywood. Such things as plot worry Saroyan not at all. People are the grist for his mill, and the Macauleys of Ithaca, Calif. are good grist. Saroyanesquely naive one moment, they are profound the next; now smug and annoying, now simple and novable....

The sum total of these screen adventures never quite attains the soaring enthusiasm of Saroyan's novel, and some of the preaching is hard to take. Yet at its best *The Human Comedy* is immensely moving. Even its preaching sometimes achieves an eloquence that gives the picture a psychological fifth dimension.

The Saroyan touch leaves nothing ordinary; the film is electric with the joy of life. It gets this quality partly from the acting of Mickey Rooney, who, despite some persistent Andy Hardy mannerisms, is for once something besides a show-off....

Van Johnson and friend pull KP duty.

107

Reunion in France

MGM

New York release date, March 4, 1943

Produced by Joseph L. Mankiewicz; directed by Jules Dassin; screenplay by Jan Lustig, Marvin Borowsky and Marc Connelly; based on an original story by Ladislas Bus-Fekete.

CAST: Joan Crawford, John Wayne, Philip Dorn, Reginald Owen, Albert Bassermann, John Carradine, Ann Ayars, J. Edward Bromberg, Moroni Olsen, Henry Daniell, Howard da Silva, Charles Arnt, Morris Ankrum, Edith Evanson, Ernest Dorian, Margaret Laurence, Odette Myrtil, Peter Whitney.

This was a potboiler about loyal Frenchmen in occupied Paris—an unconvincing attempt to suggest that despite the apparent collaboration by Frenchmen in high places, they were actually sabotaging Nazi efforts with great sacrifice to themselves. Joan Crawford starred as an *haute couture* model in love with wealthy, seemingly pro-Nazi industrial designer Philip Dorn, whose factories were in actuality turning out

Top stars Joan Crawford and John Wayne were teamed for *Reunion in France.*

108

Joan Crawford and John Wayne.

defective weapons for German troops. Miss Crawford's role gave her ample opportunity to appear in a number of flashy gowns. The plot of the film became ridiculously complex with the introduction of an RAF pilot, played by none other than very American John Wayne, whose plane was downed in France.

TIME:

Reunion in France . . . is a Joan Crawford version of the fall of France.

THE NEW YORK TIMES:

If *Reunion in France* is the best tribute that Hollywood can muster to the French underground forces

Henry Daniell and John Wayne.

John Wayne, Joan Crawford, and
Philip Dorn.

of liberation, then let us try another time. [This film is] simply a stale melodramatic exercise for a very popular star. In the role of a spoiled rich woman who finds her "soul" in the defeat of France, Joan Crawford is adequate to the story provided her....

On the basis of evidence to date, MGM seems somewhat off-base when it infers that the initiative for a French resurrection comes from its moneyed society folk and spendthrifts; hardly an ordinary French citizen appears in the film.

...John Wayne is totally unconvincing as the American flyer.... *Reunion in France* ... has had the temerity to be glibly untruthful on serious matters. It has slipped on its own banana oil.

Theodore Strauss

NEW YORK HERALD TRIBUNE:

What MGM had in mind on making *Reunion in France* is hard to say. It could be that Miss Crawford was at a loose end.

Joseph Pihodna

Joan Crawford and Philip Dorn enjoyed luxury during the Occupation.

The cast of *The Moon Is Down* assembled for a publicity photo.

The Moon Is Down

20th Century-Fox

New York release date, March 14, 1943

Produced by Nunnally Johnson; directed by Irving Pichel; screenplay by Mr. Johnson; based on the novel by John Steinbeck.

CAST: Sir Cedric Hardwicke, Henry Travers, Lee J. Cobb, Dorris Bowden, Margaret Wycherly, Peter Van Eyck, William Post, Jr., Henry Rowland, E. J. Ballantine, Violette Wilson, Hans Schumm, Ernest Dorian, John Banner, Helene Thimig, Ian Wolfe, Kurt Kreuger, Jeff Corey, Louis Arco, Ernst Hausman, Charles McGraw, Trevor Bardette, Joan Mylong, Otto Reichow, Sven Hugo Berg, Dorothy Peterson.

The film version of John Steinbeck's novel and play about the invasion, conquest, occupation and resistance of a Norwegian mining village was, many felt, an improvement over its sources in that it was less sympathetic to the Germans, whom Steinbeck

had portrayed as occasionally afflicted with at least some human doubts and frailties. But screenwriter Nunnally Johnson and director Irving Pichel retained the overall feeling of sadness and hint of hopelessness which had permeated Steinbeck's story.

The Moon Is Down was a cool, almost detached look at the plight of an occupied country and it was perhaps its lack of both passion and romanticism which accounted for its commercial failure. War-weary audiences were tiring of war pictures and the import of this attitude was not lost on the front offices, which consequently announced plans for more musicals and escapist fare and a reduction in the number of films dealing directly with the war.

Darryl Zanuck summed up the prevailing front-office feeling: "Any story about Germany or labor slaves appalls me. Every picture yet made dealing with occupied countries, including *The Moon Is Down,* has laid a magnificent egg with the public.

I can imagine no subject less inviting to an audience than the subject of slave labor at this time. I wouldn't care if it was the greatest dramatic story ever written."

Zanuck's disappointment over the failure of *The Moon Is Down* was understandable. 20th Century-Fox had paid Steinbeck a record $300,000 for the film rights to a book which had sold nearly a million copies, and a play which, although it had run only nine weeks on Broadway, was a smash hit on the road.

TIME:

The Moon Is Down presents the cinema audience with a ready-made controversy. As novel and play, John Steinbeck's fable about a Nazi garrison's nervous breakdown in Norway kicked up a loud literary row. Were Steinbeck's Nazis softer than the real thing?

They are harsher in the movie than in the novel or the play, and so is their dramatic impact.

The chief interest, with the movie as with the book and play, lies in Steinbeck's central thesis: that Nazis are vulnerable to hatred and contempt. The more the picture attempts to make this theme explicit, the more it underlines the fact that Steinbeck's premise is questionable psychology. Conquerors do not expect

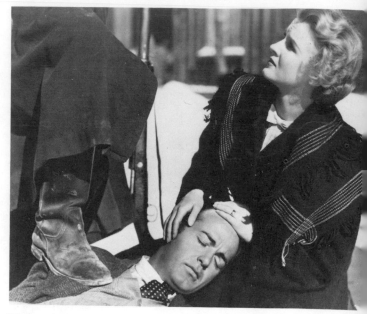

William Post Jr. and Dorris Bowden. Miss Bowden was the wife of the film's writer-producer Nunnally Johnson.

to be loved, and seldom go to pieces because the conquered fail to embrace them. *The Moon Is Down* may seem to many audiences an extraordinarily naive view of the facts of Nazi life.

William Post, Jr., at a Nazi tribunal headed by Sir Cedric Hardwicke. Also present is the town mayor played by Henry Travers.

The Nazis and Dorris Bowden. This film depicted the Nazis as almost sympathetic characters and certainly with more sympathy than did any movie of its time.

THE NEW YORK TIMES:

The noisy and passionate controversy aroused by *The Moon Is Down,* when the John Steinbeck play and novel were presented something over a year ago, is not likely to be rekindled to any appreciable degree by the clear and incisive screen version which came to the Rivoli yesterday. . . . Nunnally Johnson . . . has carefully corrected the most censurable features of the work. He has given definition at the outset to the theme—that the will of a free and noble people cannot be suppressed by violence. . . . He has wrung out such traces of defeatism as were apparent in the book and has sharpened with vivid incidents the horror of being enslaved. . . .

But the intellectual nature of this picture—its very clear and dispassionate reasoning—drain it of much of the emotion that one expects in such a story at this time. This may well be a true picture of Norway and its people. But it fails to strike fire, to generate passion. It leaves one feeling rather proud but also sad.

Bosley Crowther

NEWSWEEK:

Skillfully directed by Irving Pichel, *The Moon Is Down* doesn't rely on the melodramatics of terror and sabotage to underscore its message. More than any such film to date, this one goes beyond overt action to reach for the inner strength of a conquered people and to show, as Steinbeck concludes, that "it is always the herd men who win battles and the free men who win wars."

Dorris Bowden and Nazi soldiers.

Errol Flynn, Ann Sheridan, and Judith Anderson, Walter Huston, Ruth Gordon in *Edge of Darkness*.

Edge of Darkness

Warner Bros.

New York release date, April 9, 1943

Produced by Henry Blanke; directed by Lewis Milestone; screenplay by Robert Rossen; based on the novel by William Woods.

CAST: Errol Flynn, Ann Sheridan, Walter Huston, Nancy Coleman, Tom Faddon, Judith Anderson, Helmut Dantine, Ruth Gordon, Charles Dingle, John Beal, Roman Bohnen, Helene Thimig, Monte Blue, Dorothy Tree, Richard Fraser, Morris Carnovsky, Art Smith, Henry Brandon, Tonio Selwart, Torben Meyer.

Very soon after Fox's *The Moon Is Down* came this Warners' story of occupied Norway. As adapted for the screen by Robert Rossen and directed by Lewis Milestone, *Edge of Darkness* was an eloquent and touching tribute to Norwegian courage during the Nazi occupation. Errol Flynn was fine as the leader of a revolt in a small Norwegian fishing village, but

Ann Sheridan, complete with voguish snoods, seemed miscast as an embattled patriot. While Flynn and Sheridan were obviously the names that mattered at the box office, the supporting cast—including Walter Huston, Judith Anderson and Ruth Gordon—gave the film its moments of believability.

Edge of Darkness was plagued by problems during its production: Ann Sheridan parted from husband George Brent; Errol Flynn was indicted for rape; location shooting in a small California town was delayed several weeks because of fog, during which Ruth Gordon and Judith Anderson were besieged with telegrams from Katharine Cornell demanding their return to New York for her stage production of *The Three Sisters*. Miss Gordon was restrained from leaving, but not before letting it be known that she hated Hollywood and the picture. Fortunately for Warners, the fog lifted, Flynn was acquitted, and the film was completed.

John Beal, Ann Sheridan, and Walter Huston.

Helmut Dantine played a Nazi soldier in *Edge of Darkness*.

THE NEW YORK TIMES:

... If its conflict is simple and direct and if Errol Flynn, Ann Sheridan and others in it seem odd sort of folk for Norway, it is still a finely jointed motion picture in the craft ways of Hollywood. ...

... An account of mass resistance slowly growing about one central point until, armed with guns from England, the whole village is able to strike. ... The final, climactic battle between the Nazis and the villagers is a pip; so many have not fallen so graphically since the United States Cavalry and Mr. Flynn died very gallantly with their boots on back there at the Little Big Horn.

As a Hollywood picture about Norway, *Edge of Darkness* gets across some salient points, despite a few silly inconsistencies. ... And it concludes with a ringing transcription from President Roosevelt's "look-to-Norway" speech. But basically it is ... only a surface conception of the complicated tragedy of Norway.

Bosley Crowther

NEWSWEEK:

... While William Woods' novel of the Norwegian underground was accused—like Steinbeck's *The Moon Is Down*—of an unfortunately sympathetic consideration of the Nazi character, Robert Rossen's film adaptation recasts the enemy as an evil and ruthless monster. The resulting melodrama, while obvious, is tense, hard-hitting, and even tough enough to subject Miss Sheridan to a fate worse than death.

Coming late in a well-worn cycle, *Edge of Darkness* of necessity recapitulates much that is now familiar in the drama of oppression and rebellion. Yet Milestone (who regarded war with disillusion in *All Quiet on the Western Front*) is able to infuse any number of scenes with fresh emotional and melodramatic impact.

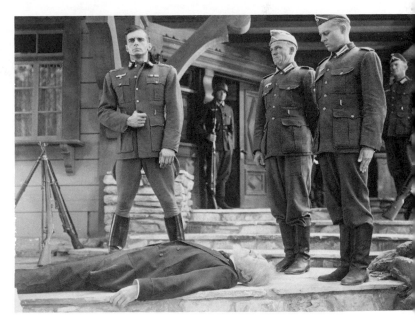

A scene from *Edge of Darkness* shows Nazi brutality in occupied Norway.

Brian Donlevy in *Hangmen Also Die*, Hollywood's version of the assassination of Heinrich Heydrich.

Hangmen Also Die

United Artists

New York release date, April 15, 1943

Produced and directed by Fritz Lang; screenplay by John Wexler; adaptation and original story by Bert Brecht and Fritz Lang.

CAST: Brian Donlevy, Walter Brennan, Anna Lee, Gene Lockhart, Dennis O'Keefe, Alexander Granach, Margaret Wycherly, Nana Bryant, Billy Roy, Hans V. Twardowski, Tonio Selwart, Jonathan Hale, Lionel Stander, Byron Foulger, Virginia Farmer, Louis Donath, Sarah Paddon, Edmund MacDonald, George Irving, James Bush, Arno Frey, Lester Sharpe, Arthur Left, William Farnum, Reinhold Schuenzel.

With the assistance of the Czech government-in-exile, and material from its files, director Fritz Lang and co-author Bertolt Brecht created a gripping story

Anna Lee.

116

about the events surrounding the assassination of Reinhard Heydrich, Reich protector (governor) in Bohemia and Moravia, and the subsequent persecutions of the unfortunate Czechoslovakians who were accused of complicity in the act.

In searing terms the film depicted the stubborn and heroic resistance of the Czechs against their Nazi oppressors. Lang kept the film shifting from the efforts of the Gestapo to locate the killer to the activities of the Czech partisans and to the irony of the "Quisling" who, though loyal to the Germans, is blamed for the crime and executed by the Gestapo in order to get their superiors off their backs.

THE NEW YORK TIMES:

. . . In so far as the picture tries to echo the anguished heroism of a captive people it fails badly both in the script and in the performance . . . [the characters of the] patriots seem postured and insufficiently sincere, their words have the hollow ring of Hollywood. . . . *Hangmen Also Die* is not the high tribute to courage it might have been; it has been too content to be merely theatrical.

Theodore Strauss

NEW YORK HERALD TRIBUNE:

The director has gone to great pains in exposing the Nazi methods of obtaining information from unwilling persons. He keeps three sub-plots spinning without too much effort and at a leisurely pace. . . . *Hangmen Also Die* is a director's picture, indelibly marked by Lang's craftsmanship.

Joseph Pihodna

Jonathan Hale and Brian Donlevy in Fritz Lang's *Hangmen Also Die*.

NEWSWEEK:

The time is coming when the cinematic celebration of a vanquished nation's resistance to the Nazis will have lost most of its dramatic impact by dint of unending repetition. That time has not yet come for such an authentic and uncompromising hymn of hate as United Artists' *Hangmen Also Die*. The first feature film to speculate on the fate of the unknown patriot who pumped three bullets in the slimly sinister figure of Reinhard (The Hangman) Heydrich . . . is both a gripping melodrama and a grimly documented indictment of the Nazi formula for conquest.

Brian Donlevy.

Brian Donlevy.

Rosalind Russell, pictured here with Herbert Marshall, played Amelia Earhart in *Flight For Freedom*.

Flight for Freedom

RKO

New York release date, April 15, 1943

Produced by David Hempstead; directed by Lothar Mendes; screenplay by Oliver H. P. Garrett and S. K. Lauren; adaptation by Jan Murfin; based on a story by Horace McCoy.

CAST: Rosalind Russell, Fred MacMurray, Herbert Marshall, Edward Ciannelli, Walter Kingsford, Damian O'Flynn, Jack Carr, Matt McHugh, Richard Loo, Charles Lung.

Rosalind Russell played flyer Tonie Carter in this thinly disguised cinematic conjecture on the disappearance of Amelia Earhart during an attempted around-the-world flight in 1937.

According to the film, Miss Carter/Earhart, hopelessly in love with reckless, feckless fellow-flyer Fred MacMurray, was asked by the Navy to fake an accident during her flight and thereby provide an excuse for a search that would enable Naval reconnaisance of suspected Japanese fortifications in the South Pa-

cific. On her flight, Tonie herself spots the fortifications but also discovers that the Japanese are on to her ruse. She bravely crashes her plane to make the Navy search possible.

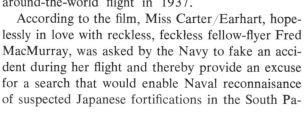

Rosalind Russell and Fred MacMurray.

118

Herbert Marshall and Fred MacMurray.

Although RKO didn't confirm or deny that the movie was based on the story of Miss Earhart, they did pay her husband George Palmer Putnam, $7,500 for his permission to make the film.

THE NEW YORK TIMES:

The strange disappearance of Amelia Earhart in the South Pacific some six years ago while circling the globe in her airplane established a mystery which has never been clarified.... Wild explanations have been advanced for the lady's vanishment . . . currently popular is that she fell into the hands of the Japs. The notion is that she spotted their forts on the mandated isles, which was strictly against League agreements, so the Japs put her permanently away....

. . . The notion is sufficiently provocative to have called forth a motion picture based on that general idea.... Mostly it is a routine story of one of those unsatisfactory romances....

Rosalind Russell and Fred MacMurray.

Rosalind Russell plays the lady with an excess of stars in her eyes and Fred MacMurray plays the gentleman with almost painful nonchalance....

The film loudly and recklessly asserts that our present naval actions in the Pacific have been made possible because of "one pretty girl." If she hadn't done this thing, it asks us, where would we be today? The question is strictly rhetorical. You either trust your ears or your good sense.

Bosley Crowther

TIME:

. . . The film makes a good technical try for pace, but never really achieves it. Russell's and MacMurray's thanks-for-the-memory love junket is as bland as anything the Hays office has swallowed in recent months. But mainly the picture is as uneven as a war-torn corduroy road.

Herbert Marshall, Rosalind Russell, and Fred MacMurray in *Flight For Freedom*, which purported to solve the mystery of Amelia Earhart's disappearance in the South Pacific.

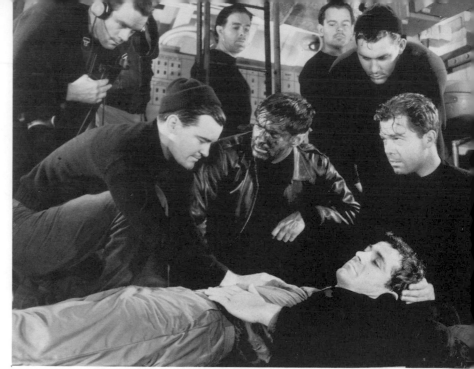

Tyrone Power, Dana Andrews in
Crash Dive.

Crash Dive

20th Century-Fox

New York release date, April 28, 1943

Produced by Milton Sperling; directed by Archie Mayo; screenplay by Jo Swerling; based on an original story by W. R. Burnett.

CAST: Tyrone Power, Anne Baxter, Dana Andrews, James Gleason, Dame May Whitty, Henry Morgan, Ben Carter, Charles Tannen, Frank Conroy, Florence Lake, John Archer, George Holmes, Minor Watson, Kathleen Howard, David Bacon, Stanley Andrews, Paul Burns, Gene Rizzi.

Crash Dive marked Tyrone Power's last pre-service

Dana Andrews, Tyrone Power and men of the U.S. Navy.

Tyrone Power in his last film before entering the Air Corps.

Tyrone Power and fellow seamen.

screen appearance. An account of modernized swash-buckling, set in the hotly contested North Atlantic battlefield, the film cast Power as a naval two-striper, a specialist in naval warfare both on and under the sea in PT boats and submarines. It also cast Anne Baxter as the girl caught in a love triangle with Power and sub captain Dana Andrews. The rather routine romantic subplot slowed down the film considerably, but the excellent action sequences and Technicolor photography redeemed it.

THE ·NEW YORK TIMES:

. . . One of those films which have no more sense of reality about this war than a popular song. . . . Such incredible heroics have seldom been seen on the screen. It is Hollywood at its wildest. And in Technicolor, too! Oh, boy! . . . It leaves one wondering blankly whether Hollywood knows that we're at war.

Bosley Crowther

NEW YORK HERALD TRIBUNE:

[Tyrone Power's] latest vehicle is . . . generally effective, and it is to be hoped, in passing, that Mr. Power's career as an officer in the Marine Corps will be as brilliant as that portrayed in his new screen offering.

The final, climactic scene, in which one of our submarines attacks an enemy base, is tops in the field of film melodrama. . . .

Otis L. Guernsey, Jr.

TIME:

. . . a Technicolored submarine story which should appeal to the boy in every man who wants to be an officer and a gentleman. The best parts of the film are its scenes of serious submarine business.

NEWSWEEK:

This goes down to the sea in Technicolor to eulogize a branch of our armed services that has had less than its deserved shares of Hollywood's attention.

Tyrone Power, Dana Andrews and sailors.

Walter Huston, center, as Ambassador Joseph E. Davies, in a diplomatic huddle in *Mission to Moscow*.

Mission to Moscow

Warner Bros.

New York release date, April 29, 1943

Produced by Robert Buckner; directed by Michael Curtiz; screenplay by Howard Koch; based on the book by former Ambassador Joseph E. Davies.

CAST: Walter Huston, Ann Harding, George Tobias, Oscar Homolka, Eleanor Parker, Richard Travis, Helmut Dantine, Victor Francen, Jerome Cowan, Henry Danieli, Barbara Everest, Roman Bohnen, Maria Palmer, Minor Watson, Moroni Olsen, Felix Basch, Kurt Katch, Leigh Whipper, Gene Lockhart, Kathleen Lockhart, Vladimir Sokoloff, Frank Puglia, John Abbott, Dudley Field Malone, Manart Kippen, Doris Lloyd, Frank Reicher, Daniel Ocko, Konstantin Shayne, Ivan Trisault, Peter Goo Chong, Lumsden Hare.

In a prologue to *Mission to Moscow* former U.S. Ambassador to Russia Joseph E. Davies appeared on screen to introduce the film version of his book and make a few remarks about why he had written his account of the two years he spent in the Soviet Union.

In the film proper, Walter Huston played the ambassador who went to Moscow, became friendly with the Russian leaders and witnessed how they were cognizant of German perfidy and the Nazi menace long before the leaders of the rest of the world. The film also stressed the similarities between the American and Russian people and it was regarded as pro-Russian propaganda—not unfashionable in those days, since Russia was then our ally. The major characters portrayed were prominent contemporary political figures, including Churchill, Stalin, Von Ribbentrop, Molotov, Litvinoff and Haile Selassie. The intention of the film was both to entertain and inform and create American rapport with the Russian people.

The film was extremely controversial in the United States, where it was attacked on the one hand as a whitewash of the Soviet regime and defended on the other as a fitting tribute to a gallant ally.

In Russia some of Hollywood's conceptions of Russian life presented in *Mission to Moscow* evoked laughter. But everyone agreed that it was excellent propaganda for fostering better relations between the United States and the Soviet Union.

NEWSWEEK:

Both as a goodwill offering and as a sincere plea for closer cooperation between the United States and

Soviet Governments, *Mission to Moscow* is notably successful. But as a clear presentation of the string of events which preceded what at the time was called the Rape of Poland, it can at the present moment be considered shy on pure objectivity.

Faced with the extremely difficult job of dramatizing a period of history that was, superficially, a war of words rather than action, Michael Curtiz deserves credit for sustaining interest as successfully as he does.

THE NEW YORK TIMES:

... A striking and controversial book, so its translation into pictures ... this generally faithful screen version ... is clearly the most outspoken picture on a political subject that an American studio has ever made.... It comes out sharply and frankly for an understanding of Russia's point of view. It says with a confident finality that Russia's leaders saw, when the leaders of other nations dawdled, that the Nazis were a menace to the world. And it has no hesitancy whatever in stepping on a few tender toes.

Particularly will it anger the so-called Trotskyites with its visual re-enactment of the famous "Moscow trials" ... puts into the record ... that the many "purged" generals and other leaders were conspirators in a plot—a plot engineered by Trotsky with the Nazis and the Japs—to drain the strength of Russia and make it an easy victim for conquest.

... It takes some healthy potshots at Britain's Chamberlain government. It characterizes the French

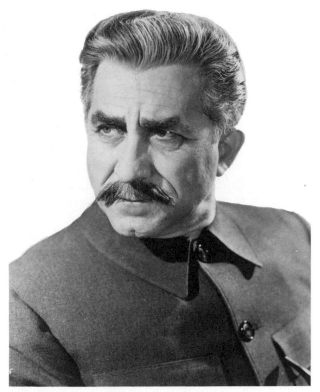

Manart Kippen as Stalin.

and Polish envoys as anti-Russian to the core and swings a vicious wallop at Congressional isolationists over here. In short, it says quite clearly that reactionaries permitted the war and that Russia, far from earlier suspicion, is a true and most reliable ally.

Bosley Crowther

NEW YORK HERALD TRIBUNE:

As an official record, *Mission to Moscow* is one of the most memorable documents of our time, because it organizes in a dramatic manner all the important political developments leading up to the war.

There is a decided Americanization of the Slavic personality and sense of values. The Russian purge trials are interpreted as a struggle between the Soviet Union and her native-born Fascists. The representatives of Germany and Japan are portrayed as incompetent caricatures of fanaticism. In these and other ways there is a simplification of history to fit an attitude.

It is good screen entertainment, and it is abundant food for thought.

Otis L. Guernsey, Jr.

Dudley Field Malone, as Churchill, confers with Walter Huston.

Charles Coburn moves in with bachelorette Jean Arthur.

The More the Merrier

Columbia

New York release date, May 13, 1943

Produced and directed by George Stevens; screenplay by Richard Flournoy, Lewis R. Foster, Robert Russell and Frank Ross; based on a story by Messrs. Russell and Ross.

CAST: Jean Arthur, Joel McCrea, Charles Coburn, Richard Gaines, Bruce Bennett, Frank Sully, Clyde Fillmore, Stanley Clements, Don Douglas.

A scene from *The More the Merrier* shows the effects of the housing shortage in wartime Washington.

Naturally, Jean Arthur and Joel McCrea wind up together in *The More the Merrier*.

Stevens' last assignment before he entered service was a merry tale, with Jean Arthur as a young Washington bachelor girl who rented half her apartment to an elderly gentleman, Charles Coburn, who thereupon sublet half of his half to a clean-cut young aviation expert, Joel McCrea. Needless to say, any number of privacy problems and slapstick situations ensued, but with Coburn as an over-aged cupid, there was a romantic resolution to them all.

Coburn really stole the show and, in fact, also walked off with a supporting-actor Oscar at Academy Award time. The film was a welcome and funny satire of a serious home-front problem.

THE NEW YORK TIMES:

... A comedy based on wartime housing conditions in Washington. . . . As warm and refreshing a ray of sunshine as we've had in a very late spring. . . . It even makes Washington look attractive—and that is beyond belief.

Bosley Crowther

NEW YORK HERALD TRIBUNE:

... The gayest comedy that has come from Hollywood in a long time. It has no more substance than a watermelon, but it is equally delectable.

Howard Barnes

This delightful home-front comedy explored with a great deal of amusement the problems of housing-bed-man-shortage in wartime Washington—a town where men were in such short supply that girls whistled whenever one passed by. Director George

Joel McCrea and Charles Coburn get carried away in a Washington nightclub.

Raymond Massey and Humphrey Bogart in *Action in the North Atlantic.*

Action in the North Atlantic

Warner Bros.

New York release date, May 21, 1943

Produced by Jerry Wald; directed by Lloyd Bacon; screenplay by John Howard Lawson with additional dialogue by A. I. Bezzerides and W. R. Burnett; based on a story by Guy Gilpatric.

CAST: Humphrey Bogart, Raymond Massey, Alan Hale, Julie Bishop, Ruth Gordon, Sam Levene, Bernard Zanville, Peter Whitney, Charles Trowbridge, J. M. Kerrigan, Dick Hogan, Kane Richmond, Chic Chandler, George Offerman, Don Douglas, Art Foster, Michael Ames, Ludwig Stossel, Dick Wessel, Iris Adrian.

This was an extended screen salute to the Merchant

Marine containing enough melodrama on the high seas for a couple of pictures. It was a moving account of the quietly heroic sailors riding "floating firecrackers" across the Atlantic, battling enemy submarines and seeing that the cargo and war material got through. Humphrey Bogart's performance wasn't up to the level of his *Casablanca* job and his part seemed rather overwritten, but the movie packed enough explosive action and spectacular effects to keep audiences entertained.

When *Action in the North Atlantic* was premiered in New York, the Merchant Marine band, seventeen torpedoed seamen and a detachment of 300 sailors marched into the theater and presented Jack L. War-

Dane Clark, Raymond Massey and Alan Hale are interviewed for radio.

ner with the service's Victory flag—the first war pennant awarded to a member of the film industry.

NEW YORK HERALD TRIBUNE:

Some of it is exceedingly impressive, as individual freighters and convoys battle to keep open the lifeline of the Allied war effort. Even with Humphrey Bogart giving a taut portrayal of a cynical mate, the film has a tendency to drag. A few reels could have been cut out of *Action in the North Atlantic* to great advantage. . . . The production has interludes of tremendous power. What is lacking is dramatic cohesion. The human narrative is highly episodic. The battles with U-boats have been well staged, but they are reiterative.

Howard Barnes

TIME:

The picture is a symphony of heaving, buckling studio sets, dubious ship-model photography and explosions on the sound track. Like many current war films, it suggests oldtime flicker serials, is directly in line of descent from *The Perils of Pauline*.

Battle-stricken ship is abandoned under fire in *Action in the North Atlantic*.

Akim Tamiroff, Franchot Tone and Anne Baxter in Billy Wilder's film about the war in North Africa.

Five Graves to Cairo

Paramount

New York release date, May 26, 1943

Produced by Charles Brackett; directed by Billy Wilder; screenplay by Messrs. Brackett and Wilder; based on a play by Lajos Biro.

CAST: Franchot Tone, Akim Tamiroff, Erich von Stroheim, Anne Baxter, Peter van Eyck, Miles Mander, Fortunio Bonanova, Konstantin Shayne, Fred Nurney, Leslie Denison, Ian Keith.

In a sort of "now it can be told" vein, Billy Wilder and Charles Brackett created a fictitious account of how the British came to win the battle of El Alamein.

It seemed that Franchot Tone, a British soldier, posing as a German agent and, abetted by a little French girl, Anne Baxter, got his hands on key secret information which enabled the British to rout the Afrika Korps of Erich von Stroheim, a.k.a. Field

Franchot Tone.

Marshall Erwin Rommel. It was, of course, purely a piece of cinematic conjecture, but an entertaining one if you didn't take it too seriously. As the "Desert Fox," von Stroheim acquitted himself with his usual Teutonic excellence. Sad to say, one of the graves was, courtesy of a German firing squad, Miss Baxter's.

Eric Von Stroheim as Field Marshall Rommel shows Franchot Tone his battle plan.

NEW YORK HERALD TRIBUNE:

...A fabulous film fable, but it has been executed with enough finesse to make it a rather exciting pipe dream.

...Pleasantly unpretentious....Tone and the other players keep their performances toned down to a pitch of muted melodrama.... Wilder is as good on desert melodrama as he proved himself earlier in the field of farce.

Howard Barnes

THE NEW YORK TIMES:

It's a good thing the German armies and Field Marshal Rommel in particular had been chased all the way out of Africa before *Five Graves to Cairo* opened ... else the performance by Erich von Stroheim of the much-touted field marshal in it might have been just a bit too aggressive for the comfort of most of us. Just as [von Stroheim] was in the last war, he is still the toughest German of them all.

Completely out of key with the performance of Mr. von Stroheim is the rest of *Five Graves to Cairo*. For otherwise it is simply an incredible comedy-melodrama....

Bosley Crowther

NEWSWEEK:

Unlike the recent run of propaganda-pregnant war films, *Five Graves to Cairo* comes under the head of entertainment, not preachment. Here is little or no fuss about Nazi ideology and democratic rebuttal. These Nazis, who have just driven the British out of Tobruk, are merely enemies who must be killed, and killed they are when the proper time comes.

Akim Tamiroff and Franchot Tone contemplate the human costs of warfare in *Five Graves to Cairo*.

Charles Laughton and Una O'Connor in *This Land Is Mine*.

This Land Is Mine

RKO

New York release date, May 28, 1943

Produced by Jean Renoir-Dudley Nichols; directed by Mr. Renoir; screenplay by Mr. Nichols.

CAST: Charles Laughton, Maureen O'Hara, George Sanders, Walter Slezak, Kent Smith, Una O'Connor, Philip Merivale, Thurston Hall, George Coulouris, Nancy Gates, Ivan Simpson, John Donat, Frank Alten, Leo Bulgakov, Wheaton Chambers, Cecil Weston.

Refugee French director Jean Renoir's second Hollywood film was set in an unidentified Nazi-occupied country that seemed much like France. Basically it was a story about how different men reacted to tyranny and of how it is sometimes the seemingly meek who make the boldest stand for liberty.

Charles Laughton played a timid, disorganized schoolmaster, who was suddenly revealed as a man of deep inner conviction and bravery when he refused to cooperate with the Nazis and, from the witness box in a courtroom, made a ringing speech about freedom. It was a speech intended not only for his

Thurston Hall and Walter Slezak.

130

Una O'Connor and Charles Laughton in *This Land Is Mine,* directed by refugee French director Jean Renoir.

Walter Slezak and Thurston Hall.

students, but spoken on behalf of all peoples in occupied lands.

THE NEW YORK TIMES:

In a sincere and responsible effort to penetrate beneath the melodramatic aspects of Nazi occupation of a foreign land and to contemplate freedom versus tyranny in terms of conflict within the human soul, Jean Renoir and Dudley Nichols have produced a sane, courageous film, marked only by occasional violences, entitled *This Land Is Mine.*

...Mr. Nichols, the author, is not concerned, as some others have been, with saboteurs and commandos, simply for melodrama's sake. His particular interest is in the fundamental nature of man and in the decisive difference between those who will submit to tyrants and those who won't.... He has bluntly indicated that the fascist-minded are in no way localized....

There are artistic faults in this picture. It is loquacious beyond excuse.... It is hard to credit the assumption on which the climax is based—namely, that the Nazis would tolerate a man speaking freely in open court. In what nation have the Germans respected the sanctity of courts?

Bosley Crowther

Thurston Hall and Walter Slezak.

131

Bataan

MGM

New York release date, June 3, 1943

Produced by Irving Starr; directed by Tay Garnett; screenplay by Robert D. Andrews.

CAST: Robert Taylor, George Murphy, Thomas Mitchell, Lloyd Nolan, Lee Bowman, Robert Walker, Desi Arnaz, Barry Nelson, Phillip Terry, Roque Espiritu, Kenneth Spencer, J. Alex Havier, Tom Dugan, Donald Curtis.

Bataan was MGM's answer to Paramount's *Wake Island*. It was a stark, tragic and compelling war drama recounting, albeit fictionally, the last days of the brave man who held on and fought to the death in order to delay the Japanese offensive on the Philippine peninsula and allow the retreating Allied forces time to make good their escape. Part of the film's power derived from its creators having given each of

Lloyd Nolan and Robert Walker in *Bataan*.

George Murphy, Desi Arnaz and Robert Walker.

the gallant but doomed thirteen American defenders individual identities and traits with which any movie-goer could empathize. Thus the men's ultimate annihilation was remembered by audiences of the day long after they left the theater, especially since superstar Robert Taylor had portrayed one of the doomed men. The losses were personal and the human tragedy of Bataan had a stunning and sobering impact.

Dore Schary points out that this was, as usual, a case where audiences identified with stereotypes. "The stereotype always appears in war pictures. Every war picture we made had a Jew, an Italian, a Pole, a WASP. But not always a Black man, because Blacks weren't integrated in the Army at that time.

"I put one in *Bataan,* just put one in, that's all. I said 'to hell with it, we're going to have one Black.' We got a lot of letters from people complaining."

THE NEW YORK TIMES:

This time . . . a studio . . . has made a picture about war in true and ugly detail. . . . It is an obviously fabricated story . . . mechanically packed with incidents, some of them moving and some of them not. . . . Tay Garnett's direction has emphasized tension much more respectably than it has framed attitudes.

The performances are consequently spotty. Robert Walker . . . is fine as the sailor. . . . Kenneth Spencer has quiet strength and simple dignity as a Negro soldier from the engineers—a character whose placement in the picture is one of the outstanding merits of it. . . .

Robert Walker and Robert Taylor.

There are melodramatic flaws in *Bataan* and it contains some admitted mistakes. But it still gives a shocking conception of the defense of that bloody point of land. And it doesn't insult the honor of dead soldiers, which is something to say for a Hollywood film these days.

Bosley Crowther

Lloyd Nolan, Robert Taylor, Thomas Mitchell, and Robert Walker.

George Murphy, Lee Bowman, Thomas Mitchell, Robert Taylor, and Lloyd Nolan.

NEW YORK HERALD TRIBUNE:

A grim and uncompromising war film. . . . Tay Garnett has staged the work with imagination and restraint. It is well and simply written and admirably performed. . . . Has heroic dimensions and a melodramatic and emotional intensity that cannot be ignored. Its tribute to the expendables who fought a desperate delaying action on a peninsula of the Philippines is as stirring as it is somber. . . .

Robert Taylor is first rate. . . . Robert Walker [is] a newcomer who is so good as the sailor stranded with an Army unit that he is certain to go far on the screen.

Howard Barnes

TIME:

Bataan's scenery is "realistic" down to the last carload of tropical foliage—and its drama is constantly loud and overemphatic. But there are a few stretches when the military situation calls for silence, the noisy sound track quiets down and, for a moment, incredibly enough, Hollywood's war takes on the tense, classic values of understatement.

The men of *Bataan,* including Thomas Mitchell, Barry Nelson, Desi Arnaz, Robert Walker, Robert Taylor. The film tried to include a soldier from each ethnic background represented in the United States.

Marsha Hunt and Franchot Tone.

Pilot No. 5

MGM

New York release date, June 24, 1943

Produced by B. P. Fineman; directed by George Sidney; original story and screenplay by David Hertz.

CAST: Franchot Tone, Marsha Hunt, Gene Kelly, Van Johnson, Alan Baxter, Dick Simmons, Steve Geray, Howard Freeman, Frank Puglia, William Tannen.

Pilot No. 5 was a story about a pilot (Franchot Tone) in the South Pacific who volunteers for a desperate mission. After he takes off, his fellow flyers wonder what motivated him to volunteer for the surely fatal task. His buddy, Gene Kelly, tells the story. In flashback we learn that early in his career as a young lawyer, Tone had become involved with a fascist-minded Huey Long-type governor in a southern state. When he finally discovered the truth about the man, he exposed him, but at the cost of his own career as well.

Determined to continue his personal fight against fascism, Tone had joined the Air Corps and become

Marsha Hunt, Franchot Tone and Gene Kelly pose for a publicity photo for *Pilot No. 5.*

Marsha Hunt, Frank Puglia, and
Gene Kelly.

a pilot in order to kill as many fascists as he could. In the film's finale, Tone, in a final act of self-sacrifice, crashes his plane, kamikaze-fashion, onto a Japanese aircraft carrier, destroying it.

Pilot No. 5 was made by MGM's "B" unit under production chief Dore Schary. The film told, in its own way, what the war was all about.

THE NEW YORK TIMES:
Throw together a group of men—on a bus, a subway or in the fighting forces—and the fiction weavers always can conjure up a tale. . . .

Pilot No. 5 is a tedious, overlong film. . . . Franchot Tone, as the misguided barrister who eventually settles his score with all exploiters of little people . . . gives an intelligent performance. Marsha Hunt, his fiancée, who saw through the governor from the start, is sweet and earnest, while Gene Kelly, the flyer who knew the whole story and tells it, is convincing.

L.B.F.

Marsha Hunt with Franchot Tone
and Gene Kelly.

Katharine Hepburn and Marjorie Riordan in *Stage Door Canteen*.

Stage Door Canteen

United Artists

New York release date, June 24, 1943

Produced by Sol Lesser and presented by Mr. Lesser in association with the American Theatre Wing; directed by Frank Borzage; screenplay by Delmer Daves; songs by Al Dubin, Jimmy Monaco, Richard Rodgers, Lorenz Hart, Johnny Green and Gertrude Lawrence.

CAST: Cheryl Walker, William W. Terry, Marjorie Riordan, Lon McCallister, Margaret Early, Michael Harrison, Dorothea Kent, Fred Brady, Marion Shockley, Patrick O'Moore, Louis Jean Heydt, Judith Anderson, Henry Armetta, Benny Baker, Kenny Baker, Tallulah Bankhead, Ralph Bellamy, Edgar Bergen and Charlie McCarthy, Ray Bolger, Helen Broderick, Katharine Cornell, Lloyd Corrigan, Ina Claire, Jane Darwell, William Demarest, Virginia Field, Dorothy

Peggy Lee sings with Benny Goodman and his orchestra.

Fields, Gracie Fields, Lynn Fontanne, Arlene Francis, Vinton Freedley, Lucile Gleason, Virginia Grey, Helen Hayes, Katharine Hepburn, Hugh Herbert, Jean Hersholt, Sam Jaffe, Allen Jenkins, George Jessel, Roscoe Karns, Tom Kennedy, Otto Kruger, June Lang, Betty Lawford, Gypsy Rose Lee, Alfred Lunt, Bert Lytell, Harpo Marx, Aline MacMahon, Elsa Maxwell, Ed Wynn, Helen Menken, Yehudi Menuhim, Ethel Merman, Ralph Morgan, Alan Mowbray, Paul Muni, Elliott Nugent, Merle Oberon, Franklin Pangborn, Brock Pemberton, George Raft, Lanny Ross, Selena Royle, Martha Scott, Cornelia Otis Skinner, Ned Sparks, Bill Stern, Ethel Waters, Johnny Weissmuller, Arleen Whelan, Dame May Whitty, and the bands of Count Basie, Xavier Cugat, Benny Goodman, Kay Kyser, Guy Lombardo and Freddy Martin.

This was a superstar-studded tribute to the American Theater Wing, which had founded and operated the Stage Door Canteen for the purpose of entertaining servicemen in New York City. The canteen received a percentage of the film's profits so *Stage Door Canteen* was in reality a big benefit staged by such theater folk as Ed Wynn, Katharine Cornell, Tallulah Bankhead, Alfred Lunt and Lynn Fontanne, Katharine Hepburn, Gypsy Rose Lee and many others who contributed their services as performers. There was a thin plot involving romance between the canteen workers and servicemen, but the use of unknowns in their parts made them relatively believeable. Stars literally tripped over one another in this highly successful pastiche, and a lot of money was raised for the actual Stage Door Canteen.

Gracie Fields.

This screen tribute to the American Theater Wing is a monster benefit in which you will find Katharine Cornell playing Juliet, Ed Wynn wearing comical headgear....Sol Lesser and Delmar Daves have contrived a neat and quietly effective production and story background for the starring acts. The stars rarely fail to deliver.

Howard Barnes

A taste of the fun and entertainment which service men share each night at the famous Stage Door Canteen. . . . A bulging and generally heartwarming film. . . . 90 per cent of the profits are to go to the support and advancement of the American Theatre Wing.

This may not be the picture to arouse the sophisticates. But it will fetch honest thrills, tears and laughter from millions throughout the land.

Bosley Crowther

. . . Hollywood's double-jumbo version of the kind of entertainment that happens nightly at Manhattan's Stage Door Canteen for men in uniform. . . . The film's patriotism is as torrential as its talents and may give civilians as well a servicemen a drowning sensation. . . .

Ethel Waters with Count Basie and his Orchestra.

Gary Cooper in Ernest Hemingway's classic story, *For Whom the Bell Tolls.*

For Whom the Bell Tolls

Paramount

New York release date, July 14, 1943

Produced and directed by Sam Wood; screenplay by Dudley Nichols; based on the novel by Ernest Hemingway.

CAST: Gary Cooper, Ingrid Bergman, Akim Tamiroff, Katina Paxinou, Vladimir Sokoloff, Arturo de Cordova, Mikhail Rasumny, Fortunio Bonanova, Joseph Calleia, Eric Feldary, Victor Varconi, Lilo Yarson, Leo Bulgakov, Frank Puglia, George Coulouris, Pedro de Cordoba, Konstantin Shayne, Alexander Granach, Adia Kuznetzoff, Leonid Snegoff, Martin Garralaga, Michael Visaroff, Jack Mylong, Feodor Chaliapin, Duncan Renaldo, Jean del. Val.

"It is a great picture, without political significance. We are not for or against anybody." So said Paramount's Chairman of the Board Adolph Zukor.

"It is a love story against a brutal background. It would be the same love story if they, the lovers, were on the other side." So said Director Sam Wood.

"We don't think it will make any trouble." So said Paramount President Barney Balaban.

"The Nazis and Fascists are just as much against democracy as they are against the Communists. They're making your country a proving ground for their new war machinery . . . so they can get the jump on the democracies." So said Gary Cooper as Robert Jordan in Paramount's version of Ernest Hemingway's controversial and very political novel about the Spanish Civil War. Cooper's remark was the only political statement in a film about the first battles between freedom and fascism.

During the film's production there had been many rumors—vigorously denied by Paramount—of political pressures and interference, presumably from representatives of Generalissimo Francisco Franco, who was touchy about being called fascist, and by American officials who perhaps did not want to offend neutral Spain.

The film, like Hemingway's novel, was the story

of Robert Jordan (played by Cooper), an American saboteur whose mission was to breach the "Nationalist" (Paramount's term for the fascist forces of Franco) lines, blow up a bridge and expedite a "Republican" (Loyalist) offensive. Cooper was perfect in his role, and Ingrid Bergman was intense and effective as the Spanish waif, Maria, a girl who had been raped and orphaned by fascist soldiers. The acting was superb throughout, and Greek actress Katina Paxinou won an Academy Award as Best Supporting Actress for her portrait of a tough, earthy guerrilla.

For Whom the Bell Tolls received tremendous prerelease publicity because of its potentially controversial politics and public interest in whether the novel's famous scene of Jórdan and Maria sharing a sleeping bag would be transferred to the screen. The sleeping bag was in but no one could tell whether the lovers were in or out of it, so skillfully photographed was the sequence.

What many had anticipated as a strong statement about the nature of the struggle of the democracies against the fascist regimes was ultimately a disappointment in its middle-of-the-road political stance, but it was, nevertheless, an engrossing love story, filled with drama and action.

THE NEW YORK TIMES:

With such fidelity to the original that practically nothing was left out except all of the unmentionable language and the more intimate romantic scenes, Ernest Hemingway's wonderful novel of the Spanish civil war . . . has been brought to the screen in all its richness of color and character. . . . The political sympathics of thc characters are perfectly clear. The protagonists are plainly anti-fascists. . . . However, the political confusion and ramifications of the civil war are as vague and strangely amorphous as they were in Mr. Hemingway's book.

Bosley Crowther

TIME:

. . . The tremendous "Bell," upon whose casting Paramount had spent three years and nearly three million dollars, tolled for nobody in particular, and tolled off key at that. . . .

The lovers and guerrillas and actions in Ernest Hemingway's novel were motivated and given their meaning by political intensities and by depths of human strength, weakness and need which Paramount has seen fit, or been forced, to remove. . . .

Paramount must be credited, to be sure, with letting Mr. Cooper murmur the no longer sensational news that Spain was a training ground for World War II. But that is about as impressive as the hindsight volubility of an upside-down parrot. Considering the particular hour and climate of world history which the "Bell" dramatizes, Paramount's executives have kept an almost divine political detachment.

NEWSWEEK:

In general, it is advisable to regard *For Whom the Bell Tolls* as a poignant, ill-starred romance, played against a grimly melodramatic background. Even here, though, the film leaves a good deal to be desired. Director Sam Wood does manage to whip the action into a superb fury of excitement and suspense in his scenes of carnage . . . and in El Sordo's gallant, hopeless delaying action on a vulnerable mountain top. Yet such moments only infrequently break a series of garrulous, though artistically arranged, close-ups in a story that lacks the variety to sustain its excessive running time. . . .

. . . For reasons that are immediately apparent, costars Bergman and Cooper were the author's choice for the principal roles; it is hard to imagine an improvement in either characterization. Yet it is the film's supporting performances that maintain its grip on the earthy realities involved.

Possibly because she is the best-realized character in the book, Pilar dominates the film. . . . Almost as good is Akim Tamiroff's surly, subtle characterization of the brutish unpredictable Pablo. . . .

Katina Paxinou, Ingrid Bergman, and Gary Cooper. Miss Paxinou won the Oscar as best supporting actress.

George Murphy.

This Is the Army

Warner Bros.

New York release date, July 28, 1943

Produced by Jack L. Warner and Hal B. Wallis; directed by Michael Curtiz; screenplay by Casey Robinson and Captain Claude Binyon; based on Irving Berlin's stage show, *This Is the Army;* music and lyrics by Irving Berlin.

CAST: George Murphy, Joan Leslie, George Tobias, Alan Hale, Charles Butterworth, Doroles Costello, Una Merkel, Stanley Ridges, Rosemary De Camp, Ruth Donnelly, Dorothy Paterson, Frances Langford, Gertrude Niesen, Kate Smith, Ilka Gruning, Lieut. Ronald Reagan, Sgt. Joe Louis, Tech. Sgt. Tom D'Andrea, Sgt. Julie Oshins, Sgt. Robert Shanley, Corp. Herbert Anderson, Irving Berlin, 1st Sgt. A. Anderson, M/Sgt. Ezra Stone, S/Sgt. Jas. Burrell, Sgt. Ross Elliott, Sgt. Alan Manson, Sgt. John P. Mendes, Sgt. Earl Oxford, Sgt. Philip Truez, Cpl. James MacColl, Cpl. R. Magelssen, Cpl. Tileston Perry, Pfc. Joe Cook, Jr., Pfc. Larry Weeks, The Allon Trio.

Alan Hale, George Murphy, and George Tobias.

The proceeds from this film version of the 1942 Irving Berlin-U.S. Army musical stage hit were turned over to an Army Emergency Relief.

The 350 soldiers who had appeared in the stage show on Broadway were in the film along with an all-star Warner Bros. cast. Berlin, who handled the musical direction for the picture, also put in a brief on-screen appearance singing "Oh, How I Hate to Get Up in the Morning."

In line with the benefit nature of the production, Warner Bros. took only enough of the gross to cover production costs. Director Michael Curtiz, author-composer Berlin and many of the principals involved donated their services, while the men who did most of the work received their regular soldiers' pay.

This Is the Army was a tremendous hit and a rousing patriotic paean to democracy, the U.S.A. and the U.S. Army.

THE NEW YORK TIMES:

This Is the Army is still the freshest, the most endearing, the most rousing musical tribute to the American fighting man that has come out of World War II. If anyone had qualms about the transfer of the stage show to the screen let him go to the Hollywood and cheer with the rest of the audience. For

Ronald Reagan.

Irving Berlin performs "Oh, How I Hate to Get Up in the Morning" in *This Is the Army*.

Joan Leslie provided the love interest for Ronald Reagan in *This Is the Army*.

Tom D'Andrea (right) and pal.

This Is the Army is that kind of entertainment—buoyant, captivating, as American as hot dogs or the Bill of Rights. It is in its way a warmly reassuring document on the state of the nation; it should frighten our enemies more than dire threat or epithet. It is, from beginning to end, a great show. . . .

There is a song for every doughboy mood—rueful, "Oh, How I Hate to Get Up in the Morning"; nostalgic, "I Left My Heart at the Stage Door Canteen"; bracing, "This Is the Army, Mr. Jones"; the wistful "I'm Getting Tired So I Can Sleep." . . .

It has the unslackening tempo and the high-hearted spirit of a country that can keep its songs and its humor even in a war. It should be G.I. for every American man, woman and child.

Theodore Strauss

TIME:

This Is the Army on Technicolored celluloid should make the flesh version's $1,951,045.11 (earned for Army Emergency Relief) look like eleven cents in a deserving bucket.

If there is an exception worth taking, it is to Warner Bros.' continued public rumbleseating with the President of the United States. It is still any gossip's guess whether the engagement is official or whether they just like each other very, very much. But when, in two pictures so close together as *Mission to Moscow* and *This Is the Army,* the President is referred to with such breath-catching reverence, it seems only decent that the audience should dim the lights, steal out softly, and leave them alone together.

Ronald Reagan, George Murphy and Alan Hale.

143

Alan Curtis and Patricia Morison.

Hitler's Madman

MGM

New York release date, August 27, 1943

Produced by Seymour Nebenzal; directed by Douglas Sirk; screenplay by Peretz Hirshbein, Melvin Levy and Doris Malloy; based on an original story by Emil Ludwig and Albrecht Joseph.

CAST: Patrician Morison, John Carradine, Alan Curtis, Ralph Morgan, Ludwig Stossel, Howard Freeman, Edgar Kennedy, Al Shean, Elizabeth Russell, Jimmy Conlin, Blanche Yurka, Jorja Rollins, Victor Kilian, Johanna Hofer, Wolfgang Zilzer, Tully Marshall.

Hitler's Madman missed no opportunity to heap terror upon terror, brutality upon brutality, culminating with the final depiction of the razing of Lidice, a small Czech town whose citizens were suspected of harboring the assassin of Reinhard Heydrich. (Heydrich's death had been dealt with earlier by Fritz Lang in *Hangmen Also Die*.) But no one who saw

Patricia Morison and Alan Curtis.

A scene from *Hitler's Madman*.

Hitler's Madman was based on a true story of the Nazi razing of a Czech town.

the film could avoid being horrified and angered by the monstrous deeds of the Nazis as they brutalized and finally massacred the hapless villagers.

THE NEW YORK TIMES:

. . . Here in one lurid diatribe, MGM's assortment of authors have summed up practically every indictment against the Nazis that they could crowd into one film.

. . . Even in its poorly depicted scenes of brutality, *Hitler's Madman* inflames a common anger. . . . As a film, *Hitler's Madman* is tritely constructed and badly played, with the exception of John Carradine. . . . In its excess of horror the film has substituted shock for moral suasion and sensationalism for earnestness. It lacks the deep fire, the grim conviction, the unspeakable resentment that will one day confront the architects of all this savagery.

Theodore Strauss

NEW YORK HERALD TRIBUNE:

. . . A horror film with few of the pleasant chills that usually accompany that type of entertainment. The only humor in the production is afforded by the ironic acting of those who play the part of Nazis in Czechoslavakia, particularly by the often-repeated line: "He died for the Fuehrer."

Douglas Sirk directed the production with skill, keeping propaganda overtones before the audience by letting the story speak for itself. John Carradine as the vicious Heydrich is excellent and Ralph Morgan acquits himself well as the timid Hanka. . . . Newspaper accounts of the bombing of Nazi cities will be pleasant antidotes for the unhappy feeling brought on by the final grim scenes of *Hitler's Madman*.

W. H.

The extras in *Hitler's Madman* included a very young Ava Gardner (fourth from right).

Bette Davis and Paul Lukas.

Watch on the Rhine

Warner Bros.

New York release date, August 27, 1943

Produced by Hal B. Wallis; directed by Herman Shumlin; screenplay by Dashiell Hammett from the stage play by Lillian Hellman.

CAST: Bette Davis, Paul Lukas, Geraldine Fitzgerald, Lucile Watson, Beulah Bondi, George Coulouis, Donald Woods, Henry Danieli, Donald Buka, Eric Roberts, Janie Wilson, Mary Young, Kurt Katch, Erwin Kalser, Robert O. Davis, Clyde Fillmore, Frank Wilson, Clarence Muse.
This was the excellent film version of the brilliant 1941 Lillian Hellman play about American complacency in the face of the growing fascist menace. Dashiell Hammett, Miss Hellman's close friend, wrote the screenplay for Warner Bros.

Paul Lukas played a determined German refugee resistance leader and Bette Davis was his wife. They returned to the stately Washington home of Miss Davis' mother, Lucile Watson, to discover, among other things, a traitor in their midst.

Watch on the Rhine was a serious and sincere film with something to say about the need for vigilance and the price men pay for freedom. Perhaps it was too serious for the war-weary moviegoers who didn't turn out en masse, despite its quality and star cachet. Paul Lukas won the best-actor Oscar for his performance.

THE NEW YORK TIMES:
Out of Lillian Hellman's stirring play . . . Warner

George Coulouris and Geraldine Fitzgerald.

George Coulouris and Paul Lukas.

Bros. and Mr. Shumlin have made a distinguished film—a film full of sense, power and beauty. . . . Its sense resides firmly in its facing one of civilization's tragic ironies; its power derives from the sureness with which it tells a mordant tale and its beauty lies in its disclosures of human courage and dignity. It is meager praise to call it one of the fine adult films of these times. . . .

For the irony Miss Hellman was pointing out back there before we entered this war . . . was the fact that some people of good-will were still blind to the barbaric nature of a conflict that has shaken the world. . . . She brought the essential conflict right into a soft American home and revealed that this modern barbarism could only be checked through force and sacrifice. . . .

. . . Miss Hellman's play tends to be somewhat static in its early stretches on the screen. . . . But the prose of Miss Hellman is so lucid, her characters so surely conceived and Mr. Shumlin has directed for

Donald Woods, Paul Lukas and Lucille Watson in a scene from *Watch on the Rhine,* based on Lillian Hellman's play.

Paul Lukas (right) won the Oscar for his performance.

George Coulouris and Geraldine Fitzgerald.

such fine tension in this his first effort for the screen that movement is not essential. The characters propel themselves. . . .

. . . An ending has been given the picture which advances the story a few months and shows the wife preparing to let her older son follow his father back to Europe. This is dramatically superfluous, but the spirit is good in these times. And it adds just that

much more heroism to a fine, sincere, outspoken film.

Bosley Crowther

NEW YORK HERALD TRIBUNE

One of the best translations from the theater that it has been my privilege to see. . . . It almost never fails to be good drama, good propaganda and good movie.

Lucas keeps the picture keyed to the sort of emotional tension that one might expect from the theme. *Watch on the Rhine* is a superior film, which makes its points straight, artistically and very pertinently for the moment.

Howard Barnes

Beulah Bondi, Lucille Watson, Donald Woods.

Claudette Colbert and Paulette Goddard headed a group of nurses trapped on Corregidor in *So Proudly We Hail*.

So Proudly We Hail

Paramount

New York release date, September 9, 1943

Produced and directed by Mark Sandrich; screenplay by Allan Scott.

CAST: Claudette Colbert, Paulette Goddard, Veronica Lake, George Reeves, Barbara Britton, Walter Abel, Sonny Tufts, Mary Servoss, Ted Hecht, Dick Hogan, Dr. H. H. Chang, James Bell, Lorna Gray, Dorothy Adams, Kitty Kelly, Bill Goodwin, Mary Treen, Helen Lynd, Jean Willes, Jan Wiley, Lynn Walker, Joan Tours, William Forrest, James Flavin, Bryon Foulger, Richard Crane, Else Janssen, James Millioan, Michael Harvey, Fred Henry, Victor Kilian, Jr., Damian O'Flynn, Ray Godin, Keith Richards, Frances Morris, Mimi Doyle, Fay Sappington, Julia Faye, Isabel Cooper, Amparo Antenercruz.

Paramount's action melodrama was an honest and memorable salute to the courage of American combat nurses. The story was adapted from first-hand accounts of the fighting in the Philippines during the Japanese offensive. Set on sea and at Bataan and Corregidor, the film focused on three embattled and emotionally pressed nurses, realistically portrayed by Claudette Colbert, Paulette Goddard, and Veronica Lake.

So Proudly We Hail demonstrated how Hollywood at its best could deliver a sincere, imaginative and stern drama without romanticizing or sentimentalizing it out of the realm of believability. The scenes of the nurses working under the fire of Japanese attack were amazingly convincing and the harrowing evacuation of the beaches at Bataan in the face of withering Japanese bombardment was stunningly re-enacted.

Claudette Colbert and Ann Doran.

Paulette Goddard and George Reeves.

Veronica Lake and Claudette Colbert.

Miss Colbert is striking and poignant as the nurse who shuns romance, burns her hands to the bone in trying to rescue a surgeon, and falls asleep on her one-night honeymoon with an Army officer. Veronica Lake, without that hairdo, is very acceptable as the embittered widow of a Pearl Harbor casualty and Paulette Goddard is excellent as the third principal in the nurses' unit. . . . a newcomer, Sonny Tufts, practically steals acting honors with his portrayal of a happy-go-lucky soldier from Kansas.

Howard Barnes

. . . The performances are hackneyed. . . . Miss Colbert gives the best among the females. . . . Miss Goddard . . . plays one for all she is worth and is consequently rather incredible; while Miss Lake, with her curtain of hair rolled up, maintains an icy rigidity until she finally eliminates herself as a human bomb. . . . A strapping new actor by the name of Sonny Tufts does wonders to give credibility and warmth to the scenes in which he plays.

The basic fault in this picture is that it sets up the illusion of place but fails to maintain it with the illusion of genuine people there. And so we behold the horror of Bataan through a transparency, through the studiously disheveled glamour of the Misses Colbert, Goddard and Lake.

Bosley Crowther

So Proudly We Hail enlists three of Paramount's brightest female stars . . . in a heartfelt, but highly fictional, tribute to the Army nurses of Bataan. The three leading ladies are so comely even in coveralls that, despite all the realistic shooting, they spend most of their time fighting a woman's war.

Claudette Colbert and fellow nurses in a lighter moment from *So Proudly We Hail*.

Eddie Cantor entertains the staff.

Thank Your Lucky Stars

Warner Bros.

New York release date, October 1, 1943

Produced by Mark Hellinger; directed by David Butler; screenplay by Norman Panama, Melvin Frank and James V. Kern, from an original story by Everett Freeman and Arthur Schwartz.

CAST: Humphrey Bogart, Eddie Cantor, Bette Davis, Olivia de Havilland, Errol Flynn, John Garfield, Joan Leslie, Ida Lupino, Dennis Morgan, Ann Sheridan, Dinah Shore, Alexis Smith, Jack Carson, Alan Hale, George Tobias, Edward Everett Horton, S. Z. Sakall, Hattie McDaniel, Ruth Donnelly, Don Wilson, Willie Best, Henry Armetta, Joyce Reynolds, and Spike Jones and His City Slickers.

In the chock-full-of-stars Hollywood-cavalcade tradi-

tion of such forebears as MGM's *Thousands Cheer,* Warner Bros. whipped together all its available talent in a song-and-dance concoction relying on star names rather than plot for its popular appeal. The slim plot involved Dennis Morgan and Joan Leslie as a couple of down-and-outers trying to land parts in a charity show being produced by Edward Everett Horton and S. Z. Sakall. Eddie Cantor played a dual role as himself and also a Hollywood tour-bus driver who abets Mr. Morgan and Miss Leslie in their efforts.

The show itself, and by extension, the film, consisted of a lot of singing—by such luminaries as Bette Davis, Errol Flynn, John Garfield, Ann Sheridan, Dinah Shore, Olivia de Havilland, George Tobias, Hattie McDaniel, Willie Best and Joan Leslie, Dennis

Edward Everett Horton, Eddie Cantor, and S. Z. "Cuddles" Sakall.

Morgan and Eddie Cantor—some dancing—by Ida Lupino, Alexis Smith, Miss de Havilland and Joan Leslie and Dennis Morgan—and a little vaudeville by Alan Hale and Jack Carson.

THE NEW YORK TIMES:

... It does seem that Warner Bros. could have thought up a better device for getting their stars before the camera to do their acts than this rather testy one. But there it is. Overlook it and you have a conventional all-star show which has the suspicious flavor of an "amateur night" at the studio. But at least it is lively and genial. All the "benefit performers" have fun.... True, the manner in which Bette Davis is presented singing a song...fails to flatter the talented lady, and Errol Flynn is a bit obvious doing a barroom ballad.... But John Garfield is highly amusing singing a tough guy's version of "Blues in the Night" and Ann Sheridan gives a saucy once-over to the ditty "Love Isn't Born, It Is Made." ... Humphrey Bogart plays a quick skit which might better have been left out.... For the sake of variety, the Warners might have worked in a little more dance and a little more femininity. Too many people sing. Too few beautiful girls display their talents. It is also too much (two hours) of a show. But in straight omnibus entertainment that's what you have to expect.

Bosley Crowther

NEW YORK HERALD TRIBUNE:

... The stars do their respective turns with alacrity, the production numbers are sumptuous for these days of priorities, and there is an excellent musical accompaniment by Arthur Schwartz.... It is best when it is toying with the tiny plot which holds a series of variety acts in some sort of continuity. Cantor... contrives some funny and consecutive slap-stick interludes, mostly at his own expense. Dennis Morgan and Miss Leslie ... lend a modicum of sense to the proceedings. Most of the others in a formidable cast come and go in random fashion.... *Thank Your Lucky Stars* has an appropriate title. Without Bogart, Miss Davis and the other Hollywood headliners, it would prove a sorry little revue.

Howard Barnes

Farley Granger, Anne Baxter and Jane Withers.

The North Star

RKO

New York release date, November 4, 1943

Produced by Samuel Goldwyn; directed by Lewis Milestone; original story and screenplay by William Hellman.

CAST: Anne Baxter, Dana Andrews, Walter Huston, Walter Brennan, Ann Harding, Jane Withers, Farley Granger, Erich Von Stroheim, Dean Jagger, Eric Robert, Carl Benton Reid, Ann Carter, Esther Dale, Ruth Nelson, Paul Guilfoyle, Martin Koslesk, Tonio Selwart, Robert Lowery.

Producer Samuel Goldwyn reportedly spent about $3,000,000 in eighteen months of production for *The North Star,* a film intended to drum up American popular sympathy for our (then) Russian allies. When the political winds changed after the war, it proved something of an embarrassment to its makers, who had to "explain it" to the House Un-American Activities Committee.

The North Star was a moving story of the suffering and sacrifices of Soviet peasantry at the hands of the German invaders. The pre-war peasant existence was portrayed rather idealistically, but the war sequences were treated in starkly realistic terms, particularly one grim segment in which a Nazi doctor drains Russian children of blood for transfusion into wounded German soldiers. The film was at its best with its account of the Russian farmers' guerrilla warfare against the occupying Nazi force.

The North Star was meticulously researched for accuracy by scriptwriter Lillian Hellman, who took pains to develop the villagers as people rather than the stock symbols of the usual anti-Nazi diatribes.

THE NEW YORK TIMES:
It is a heroic picture, the force of which is weakened only by the fact that in it Mr. Goldwyn and Mr. Milestone have too freely mixed theatrical forms. The first part of the film, in which the village and its inhabitants are idyllically introduced, is distinctly in the style of operetta. There are music . . . and rollicking gaiety of the sort familiar to light-hearted peasants

Walter Huston in Samuel Goldwyn's production of Lillian Hellman's *The North Star*.

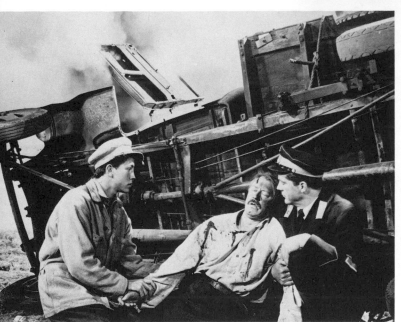

Farley Granger, Carl Benton Reid, and Dana Andrews in *The North Star,* a film later criticized as being pro-Communist.

Farley Granger, Jane Withers, Anne Baxter and Walter Brennan.

in musical comedies. . . . The contrast is therefore too prodigious when the bombs suddenly come raining down and the style of the film abruptly changes to one of vehement reality. The switch is too obvious a reminder of the theatrical nature of the film.

Bosley Crowther

TIME:

North Star tries to be a work of art. It is not. Does *North Star* effectively bring the experience of modern war to U.S. cinemaddicts, most of whom have viewed modern war only from the safe distance of some 3,000 miles? Answer: No other Hollywood film has done the job quite so well.

Humphrey Bogart and Bruce Bennett.

Sahara

Columbia

New York release date, November 11, 1943

Directed by Zoltan Korda; screenplay by John Howard Lawson and Mr. Korda; adaptation by James O'Hanlon; story by Philip MacDonald; based on an incident in the Soviet photoplay *The Thirteen*.

CAST: Humphrey Bogart, Bruce Bennett, Lloyd Bridges, Rex Ingram, J. Carrol Naish, Dan Duryea, Richard Nugent, Patrick O'Moore, Louis T. Mercier, Carl Harbord, Guy Kingsford, Kurt Kreuger, John Wengraf, Hans Schumm.

Sahara, based on an incident from the Soviet film *The Thirteen,* was a tribute to the unwavering courage and determination of the British in the battle of El Alamein. Its characters were a small group of men—soldiers of the usual mixed nationalities— wandering in the desert during the retreat from Tobruk. The film had a twofold conflict: the men not only had to find water to save their lives, but also had to defend it, as the Germans, also looking for water, advanced on the little oasis where they were holed up.

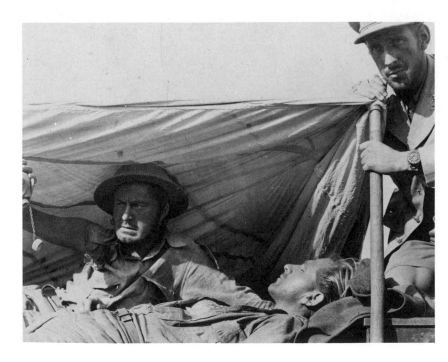

George Tobias and Lloyd Bridges.

155

The men of *Sahara,* one of the best movies about the war in North Africa.

Bruce Bennett and Humphrey Bogart.

The uneven battle of nine men against five hundred was rendered plausible by the strong position held by the small garrison and the disintegrating courage of the thirsty attacking force.

Heading the cast was Humphrey Bogart as an American sergeant commanding a tank named *Lulubelle.* The film was a cold, unrelenting statement of the brutal facts of war with almost the reality of newsreel reportage. The reality was enhanced by the use, as extras, of real soldiers who were in training at Camp Young, California, near which the picture was made.

THE NEW YORK TIMES:

All the adversities of the desert—the heat, the thirst and everlasting sand—are realized in the tortuous journey, but it is the fight against the Nazis which is tough. It is this which tests the endurance, the artifice and the spunk of the handful of Allied soldiers. And it is this which makes a tense, exciting film. . . . But it is in the fiber of the characters that Mr. Korda (and those who worked with him on the script) have accomplished some eloquent expression. Mr. Bogart is truly inspiring. . . .

Bosley Crowther

TIME:

. . . A preposterous melodrama about Humphrey Bogart, nine other heroes and a derelict tank; it is also a triumphant combination of first-rate entertainment, intelligent cinematics, and an unusual amount of honesty about war. It mixes these ingredients in a much-used shaker, according to the old Last Patrol formula.

George Tobias, Lloyd Bridges and men in *Sahara.*

Richard Jaeckel and William Bendix.

Guadalcanal Diary

20th Century-Fox

New York release date, November 17, 1943

Produced by Bryan Foy; directed by Lewis Seiler; screenplay by Lamar Trotti; adaptation by Jerry Cady; based on the book by Richard Tregaskis.

CAST: Preston Foster, Lloyd Nolan, William Bendix, Richard Conte, Anthony Quinn, Richard Jaeckel, Roy Roberts, Minor Watson, Ralph Byrd, Lionel Stander, Reed Hadley, John Archer, Eddie Acuff, Robert Rose, Miles Mander, Harry Carter, Jack Luden, Louis Hart, Tom Dawson, Selmer Jackson, Warren Ashe, Walter Fenner, Larry Thompson.

War correspondent Richard Tregaskis's best-selling book of the same title was the basis for this harrowing screen account of Marines fighting and dying in the South Sea jungles during an American offensive. While the film remained true to the spirit of the book, it used it primarily as a departure point for another Hollywood version of history which involved some varying of actual incidents for the sake of dramatic

effect. Much of the picture had a documentary-like feel about it, enhanced by the avoidance of "star" performances by any of its all-male cast.

Guadalcanal Diary followed its Marines from their pre-landing shipboard briefings through two months of hardship and fighting until they are relieved by fresh Army troops. Among its memorable characters were William Bendix, as an ex-Brooklyn cab driver; Preston Foster, as a courageous chaplain; Lloyd Nolan, as a tough sergeant; 17-year-old Richard Jaeckel, in his screen debut, as a brave youngster.

This was a stirring drama, a restrained, unromantic look at the raw face of war.

THE NEW YORK TIMES:

It opened . . . at the Roxy before an audience which was visibly stirred and which, no doubt, had the impression that it was witnessing the Battle of Guadalcanal as it was fought.

With the latter impression, we would take issue—

Richard Conte (center) in *Guadalcanal Diary*. Audiences cheered the film at the Roxy.

just on the basis of Mr. Tregaskis' book. But there is certainly no question that this picture is stirring and inspiring in many ways. . . . It has admirably stuck to the business at hand, which was fighting a war, without any pretty digressions along the incidental byways of romance.

. . . The first part of the film is almost documentarily real. . . . But, oddly enough, the sense of danger and the nightmare that lay ahead is never realized in this picture as strongly as it is in the first part. One reason is that much footage is devoted to the gags of the Marines . . . another is that the fighting is also comparatively routine, without any true indication of the tension of jungle warfare. And then, too, it seems too fortuitous that the four or five marines we stay with most enjoy a miraculous immunity from death—except for one, just at the end.

Bosley Crowther

William Bendix and men.

Richard Jaeckel and Lloyd Nolan.

TIME:

Guadalcanal Diary must be counted as much a failure as a success. With a few exceptions . . . a film which is supposed to reflect historic life and death is handicapped by too familiar faces. The picture never makes clear how desperately expendable the Marines felt on Guadalcanal. Nearly all the really deep dread and panic which developed there, and which so enhanced and complicated the bravery, is played either as simple fear or comedy. There is hardly a moment when kill-or-be-killed becomes an electrocuting fact rather than an energetic re-enactment at second hand.

Preston Foster in *Guadalcanal Diary*. The film glorified the Marines.

Nurse Joan Blondell comforts a soldier in *Cry Havoc,* another film about the courageous nurses in the armed services.

Cry Havoc

MGM

New York release date, November 23, 1943

Produced by Edwin Knopf; directed by Richard Thorpe; screenplay by Paul Osborn; based on the play by Allan R. Kenward.

CAST: Margaret Sullavan, Ann Sothern, Joan Blondell, Fay Bainter, Marsha Hunt, Ella Raines, Frances Gifford, Diana Lewis, Heather Angel, Dorothy Morris, Connie Gilchrist, Gloria Grafton, Fely Franquelli.

MGM's version of Allan R. Kenward's play, *Proof Thro' the Night,* spelled out the doom of a group of nurses caught up in the Bataan retreat. It offered a topnotch cast with Margaret Sullavan as its stalwart heroine, ably assisted by Ann Sothern, Joan Blondell, Fay Bainter, Marsha Hunt and Heather Angel. As had *So Proudly We Hail* before it, *Cry Havoc* paid tribute to the spirit of American women in terms with which any member of the audience could empathize and it made a clear comment on the value of the sacrifices women were making in the war.

NEW YORK HERALD TRIBUNE:

There is a recurring romantic contretemps between a regular Army nurse and a volunteer . . . which gets definitely tedious. . . . Obvious tear-jerker scenes, in which the nurses gradually learn that they are doomed, which are far more convincing in fact than

Marsha Hunt and Fay Bainter.

Connie Gilchrist and Margaret Sullavan.

Marsha Hunt, Heather Angel, and Ann Sothern.

the fancy of this offering. . . . The production itself is full of horror and the latent bravery that has made our enemies change their opinion about this being a "soft" nation. *Cry Havoc* is an estimable war picture, but it is still reiterative and numbing.

Howard Barnes

NEWSWEEK:

. . . The popularity that *Cry Havoc* should achieve on the screen will stem less from this probably factual record of American nurses starving, sweating, and dying in the beleaguered Philippine jungle than from the impressive all-woman cast which Metro-Goldwyn-Mayer has rounded up for the historic occasion.

Margaret Sullavan, Marsha Hunt and Joan Blondell.

Irene Dunne and Spencer Tracy.

A Guy Named Joe

MGM

New York release date, December 23, 1943

Produced by Everett Riskin; directed by Victor Fleming; screenplay by Dalton Trumbo; adaptation by Frederick Hazlitt Brennan; based on an original story by Chandler Sprague.

CAST: Spencer Tracy, Irene Dunne, Van Johnson, Ward Bond, James Gleason, Lionel Barrymore, Barry Nelson, Esther Williams, Henry O'Neill, Don de Fore, Charles Smith.

Actually there was no "guy named Joe" in this picture, but one of the characters does explain that "in the Army Air Corps, any fellow who is a right fellow is called 'Joe'."

This romantic war melodrama had Spencer Tracy get killed early on in a spectacular crash, only to return in spirit, if not flesh, to guide fledging airmen and Irene Dunne, the woman he loved, through the hazards of war. Things are okay until one of his air-

men, Van Johnson, falls in love with Miss Dunne.

The romantic rivalry brings the whole fantasy right down to earth and right down to an ending even more implausible than the fanciful life-after-life premise: Miss Dunne, with Tracy as her ectoplasmic "co-pilot," steals a plane intended for Johnson and flies off into the Pacific night on a bombing mission. Since the whole point of the film had seemed to be the importance of teamwork over individual heroics and grandstanding, it all came apart with this melodramatic turn of events.

Audiences of the day didn't seem to mind the paradoxes, however, and *A Guy Named Joe,* with its plainly sentimentalized depiction of immortality, was an enormous popular success.

NEWSWEEK:

As a war film, it combines excellent intentions and superb aerial combat shots with too much talk and

162

Irene Dunne and Spencer Tracy.

Spencer Tracy, Barry Nelson and Lionel Barrymore in *A Guy Named Joe*. The film offered a rather fanciful version of life after death.

an overcharge of sentiment. Call it a promising try that misses the boat but won't miss the box-office bull's-eye.

NEW YORK HERALD TRIBUNE:

The final sequences, in which Tracy wanders around as disembodied spirit, giving the know-all to new pilots, are strained and cinematically disconcerting. ... Dalton Trumbo has not succeeded in making this bit of metaphysical musing effective on the screen. ... [Tracy's] rivalry with a youngster who becomes engaged to his former girl is embarrassing rather than entertaining.

Howard Barnes

Van Johnson, Spencer Tracy, James Gleason and Ward Bond.

Alan Hale, Cary Grant, and crew.

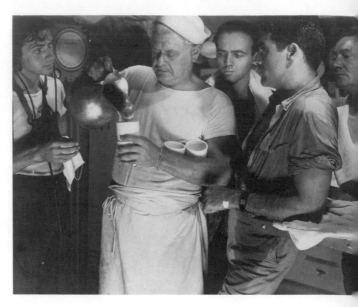

Destination Toyko

Warner Bros.

New York release date, December 31, 1943

Produced by Jerry Wald; directed by Delmer Daves; screenplay by Mr. Daves and Albert Maltz; based on an original story by Steve Fisher.

CAST: Cary Grant, John Garfield, Alan Hale, John Ridgely, Dane Clark, Warner Anderson, William Prince, Robert Hutton, Peter Whitney, Tom Tully, Faye Emerson, Warren Douglas, John Forsythe, John Alvin, Bill Kennedy, William Challe, Whit Bissell, Stephen Richards, John Whitney, George Lloyd, Maurice Murphy.

Destination Tokyo was a fitting tribute to the submarine service and an exciting account of submarine

Cary Grant, Alan Hale, and
Dane Clark.

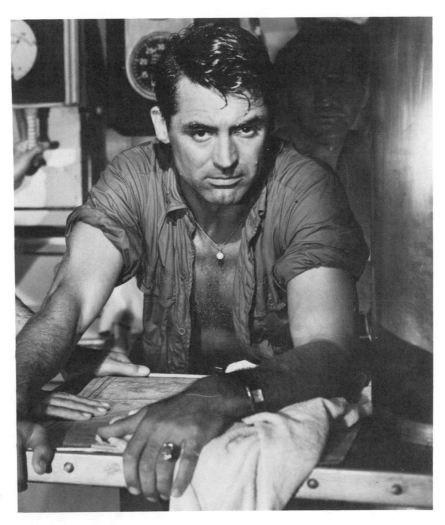

Cary Grant.

Warner Anderson and Cary Grant.

warfare. The focal point of the story was a single sub, the *Copperfin,* and her crew, captained by Cary Grant and excellently portrayed by John Garfield, Alan Hale, Robert Hutton, Dane Clark, Warner Anderson and Tom Tully among others.

The sub sails from San Francisco under secret orders to pick up a meteorologist in the Aleutians, proceed to Tokyo Bay and put him ashore so that he can provide weather information for Doolittle's raid on Tokyo. This isn't accomplished easily: the sub is attacked by a dive bomber en route and then has to navigate through mine fields before landing its passenger. There are very tense underwater moments and explosive action in an attack by the sub on a Japanese aircraft carrier. The *Copperfin* is then chased and depth-bombed by enemy destroyers before she makes her getaway.

Destination Tokyo was a successful morale-booster, powerfully combining high drama and breath-taking action.

165

Sub commander Cary Grant goes over secret orders with his crew.

Cary Grant, John Garfield, Warner Anderson and crew commend a fellow sailor's body to the sea.

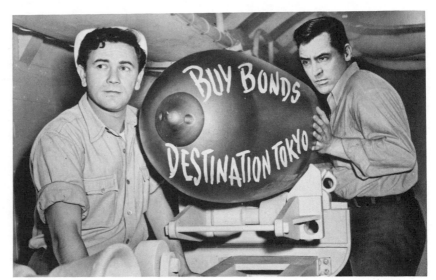

Touched-up publicity photo of John Garfield and Cary Grant for *Destination Tokyo*.

THE NEW YORK TIMES:

Everything seems to happen to the men of the sub in this case, and they rise to the challenging occasions like the heroes of Hollywood that they are.... We don't say it is credible; we don't even suggest that it makes sense. But it does make a pippin of a picture from a purely melodramatic point of view.

Bosley Crowther

NEW YORK HERALD TRIBUNE:

...So good that it adds an impressive chapter to the screen's chronicle of the present conflict. The human drama still comes through with vigor and variety in the stalwart acting of Cary Grant, John Garfield and their assistants....

Grant plays the submarine captain with his customary quizzical forcefulness, and Garfield has some fine moments of braggart comedy and sheer heroism which he handles to perfection.

Howard Barnes

The crew of the submarine *Copperfin*.

Lifeboat

20th Century-Fox

New York release date, January 12, 1944

Produced by Kenneth Macgowan; directed by Alfred Hitchcock; screenplay by Jo Swerling; based on the story by John Steinbeck.

CAST: Tallulah Bankhead, William Bendix, Walter Slezak, Mary Anderson, John Hodiak, Henry Hull, Heather Angel, Hume Cronyn, Canada Lee.

Alfred Hitchcock directed this superb screen melodrama, which approached the war from an oblique angle and emerged as perhaps one of the most pertinent and disturbing war pictures produced by Hollywood.

The action was confined to a small lifeboat adrift on the Atlantic with a handful of survivors from a torpedoed freighter. Among them was the captain of the attacking U-boat, which was also sunk during the engagement. The oddly assorted group of castaways represented a cross-section of Allied nationalities and points of view as well as personality types, including

The elements battle the inhabitants of Hitchcock's controversial *Lifeboat*.

Mary Anderson, Walter Slezak, Canada Lee, Tallullah Bankhead, and John Hodiak.

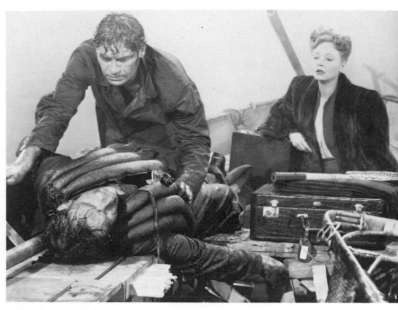

John Hodiak, Tallullah Bankhead and Hume Cronyn.

a self-centered lady journalist (Tallulah Bankhead), a bewildered nurse (Mary Anderson), a shy radio operator (Hume Cronyn), a tough crew member of Czech ancestry (John Hodiak), a shipping magnate (Henry Hull), a crazed mother (Heather Angel) and her dead baby, a black steward (Canada Lee), and a wounded crewman (William Bendix).

The film was a microcosm of the war and it was the character of the Nazi U-boat captain, excellently acted by Walter Slezak, who provided the most

Walter Slezak, Mary Anderson, Hume Cronyn, Tallullah Bankhead, John Hodiak, Henry Hull, Heather Angel, William Bendix and Canada Lee — the inhabitants of *Lifeboat*.

Canada Lee, Mary Anderson, Hume Cronyn, Henry Hull, John Hodiak and Tallullah Bankhead. Hitchcock's direction won an Oscar nomination. Tallullah won the New York Film Critics Award as best actress.

startling and controversial aspect of the picture. The Nazi was portrayed as the only stable, level-headed and practical member of the group. He was the only one among them who had a plan for survival amid the confusion and self-pity that marked his lifeboat companions. This was a disturbing factor to some critics, who were plainly alarmed at the implications. Hitchcock, however, said that he made the Nazi a strong character in order to indicate that the Nazis should not be underestimated by the Allies.

Lifeboat was a box-office success in New York City, but not elsewhere. Hitchcock received an Academy Award nomination for Best Director and Tallulah Bankhead won the New York Film Critics' Best Actress award.

THE NEW YORK TIMES:

. . . A trenchant and blistering symbolization of the world and its woes today. Within their battered lifeboat are assembled an assortment of folks who typify various strata of a free, democratic society.

In the lifeboat, also, is a German . . . personification of the Nazi creed, who proves to be the only competent leader in a boat full of ineffectuals.

Nor is [the Nazi] an altogether repulsive or invidious type. As Walter Slezak plays him, he is tricky and sometimes brutal, yes, but he is practical, ingenious, and basically courageous in his lonely resolve. Some of his careful deceptions would be regarded as smart and heroic if they came from an American in the same spot.

Obviously Mr. Hitchcock and Mr. Steinbeck failed to grasp just what they had wrought. They certainly had no intention of elevating the "superman" ideal— nor did the responsible studio, 20th Century-Fox. But we have a sneaking suspicion that the Nazis, with some cutting here and there, could turn *Lifeboat* into a whiplash against the "decadent democracies." And it is questionable whether such a picture, with such a theme, is judicious at this time.

Bosley Crowther

NEW YORK HERALD TRIBUNE:

Tallulah Bankhead comes into her own on the screen in this picture. As the well groomed and brittle commentator on world disaster who finds herself in a microcosm of catastrophe, she is supremely assured and appealing. Walter Slezak is splendid as the German.

. . . Hitchcock has . . . miraculously kept the film full of movement and a swelling mood. Here is a film to treasure among the best.

Howard Barnes

170

Anne Baxter meets Thomas Mitchell and Selena Royle, parents of *The Fighting Sullivans*.

The Fighting Sullivans

20th Century-Fox

New York release date, February 10, 1944

Produced by Sam Jaffe; directed by Lloyd Bacon; screenplay by Mary C. McCall, Jr.; from a story by Edward Doherty and Jules Schermer.

CAST: Anne Baxter, Thomas Mitchell, Selena Royle, Edward Ryan, Trudy Marshall, John Campbell, James Cardwell, John Alvin, George Otterman, Jr., Roy Roberts, Ward Bond, Mary McCarty, Bobby Driscoll, Nancy June Robinson, Marvin Davis, Buddy Swan, Billy Cummings, Johnny Calkins.

This was the true story of five brothers who fought and died together when their ship, the American cruiser *Juneau,* was sunk in the South Pacific.

The Fighting Sullivans really spent most of its time telling why the boys fought rather than how they fought. It traced their lives from boyhood in Waterloo, Iowa and was in essence a story of "typical" Americans and of love centered around home and family. Through its account of the lives of these

brave young men, the film gave all Americans a renewed sense of what the war was all about.

Thomas Mitchell and Selena Royle seemed just right as the parents of Al, Frank, George, Matt and Joe, who were all portrayed by unknown actors who gave an added feeling of realism and poignancy to the film.

The Fighting Sullivans was a simple, "small" picture which proved to be a sleeper. Interestingly, it had undergone a title change between its initial New York release and subsequent bookings. Originally it was entitled *The Sullivans* but proved to be a disappointment at the box office until the new title was appended, whereupon it became an unqualified success.

THE NEW YORK TIMES:

The real-life story of the Sullivans . . . is a deeply touching story because of the personal sacrifice it represents. . . . One might, if one chose, make the comment that the producers, in fashioning this film,

171

Selena Royle and Thomas Mitchell.

The fighting Sullivans. It was a true story.

have played rather heavily upon the obvious and have adorned their film freely with clichés. . . . But the truth often lies in the obvious. And it so happens that there emerges in this film a simple and genuine feeling for boys and for Americans as we are. The juvenile joys of the Sullivans . . . have a natural, authentic appeal. . . . This film gets down to human nature, with humor and honest sentiment. . . . Alto-gether, we can recommend *The Sullivans* as a fond and satisfying American film.

Bosley Crowther

20th Century-Fox's *The Sullivans* is something more than a worthy tribute to a pair of small-town parents and the five sons they lost when the . . . *Juneau* blew up in battle off Guadalcanal. It is also a heartwarm-

The fighting Sullivans. The film was originally titled *The Sullivans* and flopped. As *The Fighting Sullivans* it became a sleeper.

ing . . . slice of Americana that will fill in the background of any number of Americans on the fighting fronts. . . .

. . . Although audience awareness of the news in store for the Sullivan family adds considerably to the film's effect, *The Sullivans* generates emotion strictly on its own terms and without bidding for tears. Lloyd Bacon directs the script with a sure feeling for its everyday, homespun trivia, and his cast responds with understanding performances. . . .

Thomas Mitchell as the father of *The Fighting Sullivans*.

Song of Russia

MGM

New York release date, February 10, 1944

Produced by Joseph Pasternak; directed by Gregory Ratoff; screenplay by Paul Jarrico and Richard Collins; based on a story by Leo Mittler.

CAST: Robert Taylor, Susan Peters, John Hodiak, Robert Benchley, Felix Bressart, Michael Chekhov, Darryl Hickman, Jacqueline White.

Only a few years before making *Song of Russia,* MGM had satirized the Soviet Union with *Ninotchka* and *Comrade X.* In step with the changing times, the studio now made a picture with the intent of increasing American sympathy for the Russian people.

Song of Russia was a ludicrous story concerning a

The peasants, MGM-style, in *Song of Russia.* Russian audiences laughed at how they were depicted.

Robert Benchley and Susan Peters.

famous American symphony orchestra conductor, played noticeably off-tempo by Robert Taylor (in his last pre-enlistment role), who goes to Russia on a concert tour just before the German invasion. He barely has time to visit the hometown of Tchaikovsky and fall in love with a musically-inclined little peasant girl, Susan Peters, before the outbreak of hostilities forces the picture to shift its attention to the Soviet war effort. The major effect of the picture was to make one wish the Nazis had invaded earlier and spared us the embarrassment of the trivial romanticism.

A few years after the war Robert Taylor testified before the House Un-American Activities Committee, which was interested in *Song of Russia,* saying that he hadn't wanted to do the film.

NEW YORK HERALD TRIBUNE:

Neither of the two stories is particularly well presented, and nothing is gained by putting them together. . . . The love story is tiresomely long and rambles through endless local-color sequences in the little town of Tschaikovskoye, in which Russian peasand life is pictured as an improbably ideal, friendly existence. One never really believes in Mr. Taylor as a conductor, especially when his baton is out of

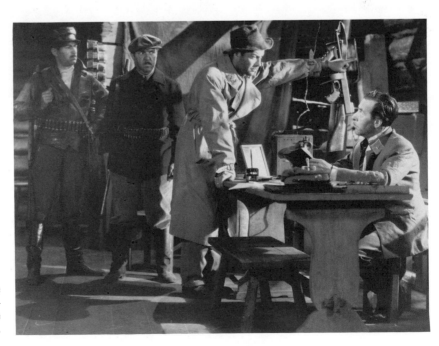

Robert Taylor in *Song of Russia.* He later testified before the House Un-American Activities Committee that he hadn't wanted to make the picture.

Robert Taylor and Susan Peters.

rhythm; nor does the clean, sweet Susan Peters become anything but an American version of a peasant girl. Their love affair is stereotyped cinema romance, and the war is a welcome relief.

The dramatization of Russia's early mobilization against the Nazis is very interesting indeed, but the romantic cliché keeps interfering with it.

Russia itself has all too little to do with *Song of Russia*.

Otis L. Guernsey, Jr.

TIME:

Many U.S. soldiers find this naive propaganda one long howl of laughter. Many civilians may find bits of it acceptable.

NEWSWEEK:

MGM performs the neatest trick of the week by leaning over backward in Russia's favor without once swaying from right to left.

Robert Taylor and Susan Peters.

Dana Andrews, Richard Loo in *The Purple Heart,* one of few films made about American prisoners of war in Japan.

The Purple Heart

20th Century-Fox

New York release date, March 8, 1944

Produced by Darryl Zanuck; directed by Lewis Milestone; screenplay by Jerome Cady; from a story by Melville Crossman.

CAST: Dana Andrews, Richard Conte, Farley Granger, Kevin O'Shea, Sam Levene, Donald Barry, Charles Russell, John Craven, Tala Birell, Richard Loo, Peter Chong, Gregory Gaye, Torben Mayer, Kurt Katch, Martin Garralaga, Nestor Paiva, H. T. Tsiang, Benson Fong, Kev Chang, Beal Wong.

Released shortly after the government's publication of reports of Japanese torture of American prisoners of war, *The Purple Heart* was extremely timely and moving.

Produced by Darryl F. Zanuck and directed by Lewis Milestone, the film was based on the story of eight crewmen of a U.S. bomber downed during the April, 1942, raid on Tokyo. The captured men were hauled into Japanese criminal court and tried for "murder" while various tortures were used to try to wring from them confessions of their guilt and information about American bomber bases.

The Purple Heart was a study in American courage and steadfastness to the end in the face of enemy brutality.

THE NEW YORK TIMES:

... An overpowering testimonial it is ... a splendid tribute to the bravery of young men who have main-

Sam Levene and Richard Conte.

Richard Loo, the Cruel Japanese general in *The Purple Heart*.

tained their honor and dignity despite the brutal tortures of the Japanese; and a shocking and debasing indictment of the methods which our enemies have used. Americans cannot help but view this picture with a sense of burning outrage—and hearts full of pride and admiration for our men who have so finely fought and died. . . . Such a story might seem harshly depressing in a film, but in this one it rings with gallant spirit and with inner nobility. . . .

Bosley Crowther

NEWSWEEK:

. . . If this film isn't the macabre McCoy, it is a reasonable approximation. Darryl Zanuck, hiding behind

Richard Conte, Kevin O'Shea, Farley Granger, Dana Andrews, Charles Russell and Sam Levene.

Benson Fong.

his favorite pseudonym (Melville Crossman), has written a plausible and shocking story of the American flyers who are charged with murder on the spurious grounds of having strafed nonmilitary objectives. . . .

Shrewdly, Lewis Milestone has elected to dramatize the torture chamber by indirection, leaving the satanic details to the imagination. Otherwise, the director has developed his somber theme with the vivid realism of a newsreel report. With Dana Andrews and Sam Levene heading his capable cast, Milestone achieves not only an expert job of moviemaking but a propaganda film that will leave you as disorganized as a haymaker to the midriff.

179

Chill Wills and Robert Walker in
See Here, Private Hargrove.

See Here, Private Hargrove

MGM

New York release date, March 21, 1944

Produced by George Haight; directed by Wesley Ruggles; screenplay by Harry Kurnitz; based on the book by Marion Hargrove.

CAST: Robert Walker, Donna Reed, Keenan Wynn, Robert Benchley, Ray Collins, Chill Wills, Bob Crosby, Marta Linden, Grant Mitchell, George Offerman, Jr., Edward Fielding, Donald Curtis, William "Bill" Phillips, Douglas Fowley.

This service comedy was a highly successful adaptation of the book by GI Marion Hargrove, who chronicled in amusing detail the trials, tribulations and triumphs of GI's in an army camp. It was an absorbing tapestry of the small adventures and misadventures which dominate the life of a soldier in the making. Hargrove was perpetually in and out of trouble—and, of course, KP duty—but of course he ultimately wound up as a first-rate soldier. Robert

Walker played the title role convincingly, and the film was a great hit with wartime audiences.

THE NEW YORK TIMES:

It may be that this joyous manifestation of fun and frolic at a basic training camp is a little bit wishful in its blinking of some of the harsher realities of war; it might be that its emphasis is slightly heavy upon the first person very singular. But Private (now Sergeant) Hargrove made the best of a solemn thing when he hit the ranks. And it may be said that Metro has done the same—or much the same—by his book.

As a chronicle of life in the Army, we would say that *See Here, Private Hargrove* is not the definitive article. But it makes a gay and entertaining film.

Bosley Crowther

NEW YORK HERALD TRIBUNE:

With Robert Walker playing Hargrove like a veteran

Donna Reed comforts Robert Walker, who's bribing Keenan Wynn.

trouper and such excellent supporting performers as Robert Benchley, Keenan Wynn, Ray Collins and Chill Wills adding a wide range of clowning embellishments to the proceedings, it is a singularly satisfying show.

. . . Harry Kurnitz has composed a fresh and funny continuity from the Marion Hargrove book and Wesley Ruggles has directed it as though he were actually reporting on a period of small adventures of basic training.

Walker has had scant experience, but you would never know it from this film. He plays the leading part boyishly, but refrains from making Hargrove a dolt.

Howard Barnes

Donna Reed played Marion Hargrove's girl.

Four Jills and Jessica. (*Four Jills in a Jeep.*)

Four Jills in a Jeep

20th Century-Fox

New York release date, April 5, 1944

Produced by Irving Starr; directed by William A. Seiter; screenplay by Robert Ellis, Helen Logan and Snag Werris; based on a story by Froma Sand and Fred Niblo, Jr.

CAST: Kay Francis, Carole Landis, Martha Raye, Mitzi Mayfair, John Harvey, Dick Haymes, Phil Silvers, Jimmy Dorsey and his orchestra, Betty Grable, Alice Faye, Carmen Miranda, Lester Matthews, Glen Langan, Paul Harvey, Miles Mander, Alec Harford, Betty Roadman, Winifred Harris.

Critics regarded *Four Jills in a Jeep* as a bald-faced attempt to capitalize on the well publicized 1942-43 U.S.O. tour of the four stars: Kay Francis, Carole Landis, Martha Raye and Mitzi Mayfair. The girls played themselves and the film went so far as to re-enact the actual romance and marriage between Miss Landis and an airman she met on the tour.

In an obvious attempt to give this corn some added—and needed—lustre, Fox assigned cameo roles to its top box-office stars Betty Grable, Alice Faye and Carmen Miranda, but no one could save it from seeming like an unabashed case of self-backslapping. Servicemen in particular seemed to dislike Hollywood's self-congratulations. In Iceland a showing of the film ended abruptly at mid-point when a crowd of GI's walked out on it.

NEW YORK HERALD TRIBUNE:

There are two definite reasons why this picture should have been left in its tin container. Primarily, its silly actual experiences, its bad acting and production and its retakes of dead and buried Fox musical numbers make it one of the dullest bits of entertainment ever. Secondarily, its self-praise, its recurrent theme of "Look what we girls did for our country" is almost sickening.

Undoubtedly the studio couldn't resist making capital on its girls' U.S.O. tour, but it has done it in the

Carole Landis and soldier.

worst possible taste. Even if the picture itself were gay it would still labor under an embarrassing lack of shame.

Otis L. Guernsey, Jr.

THE NEW YORK TIMES:

... [This] claptrap saga ... is just a raw piece of capitalization upon a widely publicized affair.... As an authentic record of that journey it may or may not have its points.... As a piece of screen entertainment it is decidedly impromptu. It gives the painful impression of having been tossed together in a couple of hours.

Bosley Crowther

Phil Silvers escorts four jills: Kay Francis, Martha Raye, Carole Landis and Mitzi Mayfair.

183

The Hitler Gang

Paramount

New York release date, May 7, 1944

Directed by John Farrow, written by Frances Goodrich and Albert Hackett.

CAST: Robert Watson, Roman Bohen, Martin Kosleck, Victor Varconi, Luis Van Rooten, Alexander Pope, Ivan Triesault, Poldy Dur, Helene Thimig, Reinhold Schunzel, Sig Rumann, Alexander Granach, Fritz Kortner, Tonio Selwart, Richard Ryen, Ray Collins, Ludwig Donath, Erno Verebes, Walter Kingsford, Fred Nurney, Arthur Loft, Lionel Royce.

Paramount's quasi-documentary of the rise and growth of the Third Reich strove more for factual accuracy than for drama in its portrait of Adolf Hitler and his minions.

Although Robert Watson was almost a dead-ringer for the Chancellor, his characterization made Hitler seem too much a mental case to have achieved and held his powerful position. The evil henchmen who surround and abet the dictator were much more believeably and convincingly portrayed. The flaws of

A scene from *The Hitler Gang.*

John Farrow directed *The Hitler Gang*.

the film do not, however, detract from its overall interest.

Producer B. G. DeSylva claimed that every scene of the script had been "authenticated from every available source," and "is true insofar as decency will permit." DeSylva had been prompted to make *The Hitler Gang* after seeing an official Nazi film and being angered by its distortion of facts.

THE NEW YORK TIMES:

Any critical approach to Paramount's *The Hitler Gang* . . . must be made on the basis of its being primarily a propaganda piece. As such, it would seem, the results are as important as the mechanism. One result is to leave the impression that Hitler, the villain in the piece, came out a more tolerable or, at least, a less odious person than did his henchmen. . . .

Robert Watson as Hitler.

... As the most complete pictorial documentation we have to date on the birth and growth of Nazism, it has a place unique, resisting comparison or qualitative judgment. Those of us, and that is practically all-embracing, who would profit by seeing, closeup, the genesis and spread of an ideological virus, would do well to see *The Hitler Gang*.

Paul P. Kennedy

NEWSWEEK:

...A grimly devastating history of the rise of National Socialism. Beginning with Cpl. Adolf Hitler as a paranoiac case in a German hospital in 1918 and closing with the 1934 blood purge, the screen play trenchantly summarizes sixteen years of murder, double-crossing, and degeneracy....

...Director John Farrow settled for restraint rather than box-office sensationalism. If the little corporal appears at times as a psychopathic clown, at least the motives of the men behind him are exposed in all their deadliness....

Betty Grable and an admirer in *Pin-Up Girl.*

Pin Up Girl

20th Century-Fox

New York release date, May 10, 1944

Produced by William Le Baron; directed by Bruce Humberstone; screenplay by Mr. Le Baron, Robert Ellis, Helen Logan and Earl Baldwin; based on a story by Libbie Block.

CAST: Betty Grable, John Harvey, Martha Raye, Joe E. Brown, Eugene Pallette, Dave Willock, Dorothea Kent, Robert Homans, Marcel Dalio, Roger Clark, Leon Belasco, Irving Bacon, Walter Tetley, and the Skating Vanities, the Condos Brothers, and Charlie Spivak and his orchestra.

Pin Up Girl is probably the quintessential musical extravaganza entertainment of the war years, the sort of nonsense, consistently popular and successful, which usually boiled down to a group of musical numbers and big stars in search of an elusive, if at all existent, plot. This was also the sort of total escapist fare civilian and military audiences flocked to, to forget their cares and be entertained by the lovely Betty Grable.

Betty Grable's films—and most of her rivals' "glamour-girl" pictures—were solid box-office hits during the war years.

Betty Grable had ample chance to show off her beautiful legs in *Pin-Up Girl*.

Martha Raye and Joe E. Brown in *Pin-Up Girl*. The film's plot was literally nonexistent.

Martha Raye clowns with bandleader Charlie Spivak.

THE NEW YORK TIMES:

Considering the cosmic importance of the so-called pin-up girl—and especially of Betty Grable in that particular field—it is plain that a picture more exalting, and more revealing of the subject at hand could have been made as a tribute to the sweet things than 20 Century-Fox's *Pin-Up Girl*.... A spiritless blob of a musical, and a desecration of a most inviting theme.

Bosley Crowther

NEW YORK HERALD TRIBUNE:

Hollywood invariably falls back on specialty acts when it lacks an honest script. It has done so in no uncertain manner in *Pin-Up Girl*.... Miss Grable tries hard as the heroine of the title, but she rarely succeeds in being the hot number she is supposed to represent....

Howard Barnes

Betty Grable, Joe E. Brown, John Harvey and Martha Raye.

Irene Dunne and Van Johnson in
The White Cliffs of Dover.

The White Cliffs of Dover

MGM

New York release date, May 10, 1944

Produced by Sidney Franklin; directed by Clarence Brown; screenplay by Claudine West, Jan Lustig and George Froeschel; based on the poem "The White Cliffs" by Alice Duer Miller; additional poetry for the picture by Robert Nathan.

CAST: Irene Dunne, Alan Marshal, Roddy Mc-Dowall, Frank Morgan, Van Johnson, C. Aubrey Smith, Dame May Whitty, Gladys Cooper, Peter Lawford, John Warburton, Jill Esmond, Brenda Forbes, Norma Varden.

Perhaps Metro-Goldwyn-Mayer was hoping for a second *Mrs. Miniver* in this attempt to stretch Alice Duer Miller's poem, "The White Cliffs of Dover," into a full-length film. Metro's hopes certainly weren't

realized, even though the acting and production were first-rate. The poem was simply too flimsy a framework on which to hang an entire film and the movie inevitably bogged down with its obviously sentimental story of the life of a courageous young American girl who marries a landed Englishman, loses him in the First World War and their son in the second.

THE NEW YORK TIMES:

When Metro-Goldwyn-Mayer extends its hand across the seas to our gentle English cousins it always does so with a fine fraternal grip. But in [*The White Cliffs of Dover*] . . . it has supplemented the handshake with a tug on the forelock and a bow. As a matter of fact, it has virtually gotten down on its knees and kissed the ground—the ground, that is, of England and all

Alan Marshall and Irene Dunne.

it represents. For this sterling-silver picture . . . is such a tribute to English gentility as only an American studio would dare to make.

She [Irene Dunne] keeps her chin up and her eyes dry when her husband goes off to the first World War, and stands stiffly by the old manor when she gets news of his death on Armistice Day. She even raises her young son to be a proper English lord. . . . And, with true sacrificial nobility, she sees her son give his life in this war, comforted by the knowledge that he has died for a lofty ideal.

For such folks as like to think of England and America being symbolically bound by such ties, say, as Lady Astor's, *The White Cliffs of Dover* should be a comforting film.

Bosley Crowther

NEWSWEEK:

Whether Metro-Goldwyn-Mayer has always done right by England is a matter of opinion, even in England, but no one can deny that the studio hasn't tried hard and often. Take *Goodbye, Mr. Chips, Mrs. Miniver, Random Harvest* and now *The White Cliffs of Dover.* . . . Anglophile though the first three pictures were, the new one is more so with knobs on. . . .

The Story of Dr. Wassell

Paramount

New York release date, June 6, 1944

Produced and directed by Cecil B. De Mille; screenplay by Alan LeMay and Charles Bennett; based upon the story of Commander Corydon M. Wassell and also upon the story by James Hilton.

CAST: Gary Cooper, Laraine Day, Signe Hasso, Carol Thurston, Dennis O'Keefe, Stanley Ridges, Renny McEvoy, Carl Esmond, Elliott Reid, Philip Ahn, Lester Matthews, Barbara Britton, Oliver Thorndike, Douglas Fowley, Miles Mander, Joel Allen, James Mullican, Melvin Francis, Edward Fielding.

During one of his "fireside chats," President Roose-

The boys camp it up in DeMille's
The Story of Dr. Wassel.

Barbara Britton supervises as one wounded serviceman shaves another.

velt told of the heroic exploits of a brave Navy doctor in the Far East. One of the millions listening to the broadcast was Paramount director Cecil B. De Mille. He immediately began a film about the doctor who had stood by eight wounded men, all stretcher cases, during the Japanese invasion of Java, and who,

against heavy odds, had managed to get all of them to Australia alive.

Gary Cooper played the quiet Doctor Wassell with a grim resolve, but the true feeling of the doctor's simple heroics became submerged amid the usual De Mille Technicolored touches—including a thoroughly banal and gratuitous romance and even danc-

Laraine Day surrounded by the Navy in *The Story of Dr. Wassell*. The critics were unanimous in their panning of the movie.

Gary Cooper, Stanley Ridges, and Carl Esmond.

ing girls. The result was an over-long cliché-ridden disaster.

NEW YORK HERALD TRIBUNE:

. . . The director has taken a true story of heroism . . . and jangled it into a cacophony of dancing girls, phoney self-sacrifice and melodramatic romance.

Howard Barnes

NEWSWEEK:

Wassel has described the film as 98 per cent docu-mentary. Nevertheless [much of the film] seems contrived and inadequate padding for one of the Pacific war's most gallant episodes.

THE NEW YORK TIMES:

. . . Mr. De Mille has fashioned a fiction which is as garish as the spires of Hollywood . . . flamboyant melodrama . . . [De Mille has] messed up a simple human story with the cheapest kind of comedy and romance.

Bosley Crowther

Dennis O'Keefe with native girl.

Dragon Seed

MGM

New York release date, July 20, 1944

Produced by Pandro S. Berman; directed by Jack Conway and Harold S. Bucquet; screenplay by Marguerite Roberts and Jane Murfin; based on the novel by Pearl S. Buck.

CAST: Katharine Hepburn, Walter Huston, Aline MacMahon, Akim Tamiroff, Turhan Bey, Hurd Hatfield, J. Carroll Naish, Agnes Moorehead, Henry Travers, Robert Bice, Robert Lewis, Frances Rafferty, Jacqueline De Wit, Clarence Lung, Paul E. Burns, Anna Demetrio.

Based on the Pearl S. Buck novel, this memorable tribute to the embattled Chinese was a stirring ac-

Walter Huston.

count of peace-loving people goaded into action by invasion but retaining throughout their ordeal their basic faith in the fundamental and enduring aspects of life.

Despite the varied accents of Katharine Hepburn, Walter Huston, Aline MacMahon, Turhan Bey and Akim Tamiroff, audiences accepted them as Chinese farmers engaged in a desperate struggle against the occupying Japanese. The film dealt directly with the holocaust of invasion as it affected the inhabitants of a small valley near a city. Here typical peasants, whose family life was vividly described, had lived in disregard of the outside world until the conquerer came. The inevitable traitor reared his head and the young turned to guerrilla warfare for the sake of their country. Particularly touching was the moment when the farmers put their fields to the torch rather than allow them to benefit the Japanese.

NEW YORK HERALD TRIBUNE:

. . . (A) fine and forthright film. . . . While it deals with the rape of a peaceful and isolated Chinese community, it holds to a splendid over-all document of the things free men are fighting for in these terrible days . . . the pattern of the whole war is caught inextricably in the exposition.

Aline McMahon and Walter Huston.

Katharine Hepburn.

196

Katharine Hepburn and Turhan Bey.

... Miss Hepburn gives a beautifully modulated performance of Jade, taking her husband into the guerrilla camp, destroying traitors and invaders and sending her son to safety in unconquered China so that she may keep up the good fight.

Howard Barnes

THE NEW YORK TIMES:

There are moments when the audience feels or, at the least, almost feels the real immensity of the theme, that of a big, lumbering nation being stabbed and slashed and humiliated by inecorable and vicious little men.

... The picture's great weakness lies in its failure to produce characterizations as strong and as faithful as the over-all structure.

P.P.K.

NEWSWEEK:

Though following avidly Pearl Buck's measured novel of the same name, *Dragon Seed* loses every opportunity for powerful drama.... Tight-lipped in her role of Jade, the ... freethinking wife, Miss Hepburn reveals a fine understanding particularly in those moments when she finds courage to drop her Bryn Mawr accent.

Walter Huston and family, including Katharine Hepburn, Aline McMahon, Hurd Hatfield and Turhan Bey.

197

Jennifer Jones, Joseph Cotten, Robert Walker, and Claudette Colbert in Selznick's blockbuster, *Since You Went Away*.

Since You Went Away

United Artists

New York release date, July 20, 1944

Produced by David O. Selznick; directed by John Cromwell; screenplay by Mr. Selznick; based on the book by Margaret Buell Wilder.

CAST: Claudette Colbert, Jennifer Jones, Shirley Temple, Hattie McDaniel, Jane Devlin, Lloyd Corrigan, Monty Woolley, Agnes Moorehead, Joseph Cotten, Robert Walker, Guy Madison, Adeline de Walt Reynolds, Lionel Barrymore, Craig Stevens, Albert Basserman, Nazimova, Jimmy Clemons, Jr., Keenan Wynn, Jackie Moran, Addison Richards.

David O. Selznick's epic account of civilian life during wartime was nearly three hours long. It was the story of a year (1943) and of the things that happened during that year to the inhabitants of "that fortress, the American Home."

Since You Went Away enshrined the "typical" all-American family—Claudette Colbert, the mother; Jennifer Jones and Shirley Temple, her daughters; Hattie McDaniel, their maid; and Soda, their pet bulldog. All of them were keeping the home fires burning while the man of the house was off fighting the war. Their hopes and fears and troubles mirrored those of the nation and the film, without once cutting away to battle scenes, built up a remarkable sense of the struggle Americans were involved in.

Selznick's picture celebrated the courage of American families much as *Mrs. Miniver* had paid homage to the English. It too was a blockbuster and grossed over $4 million.

THE NEW YORK TIMES:

For two hours and fifty-one minutes this new film . . . delves with a warm and gracious sympathy into the heart of what it terms "the American home" and yearns with a mother and her daughters whose best-loved men go dutifully to war . . . its spirit is hopeful and brave. But it does come off, altogether, as a rather large dose of choking sentiment.

From a mild little volume of letters . . . letters supposedly written by a wife to her husband off at war . . . [Selznick] has gathered some fragments of story and magnified them into a towering tale of one mid-West family's experiences under the abnormal strains of war.

As a typical American family, the one which Mr. Selznick has devised might be seriously questioned, however—except as a radiant ideal.

No doubt, this would have been a sharper picture if Mr. Selznick had played it in much less time, and it would have been considerably more significant had he kept it somewhat closer to average means.

Bosley Crowther

Joseph Cotten and Claudette Colbert.

NEW YORK HERALD TRIBUNE:

Since You Went Away jerks at one's tear ducts in no uncertain manner. It is overlong and episodic and it takes some license, to my way of thinking, with the obvious tragedy of war, but it has heart and a curious simplicity which permits each and every spectator to identify himself with a screen fable.

TIME:

What makes *Since You Went Away* sure-fire is in part its homely subject matter, which has never before been so earnestly tackled in a film. . . . Though idealized, the Selznick characterizations are authentic to a degree seldom achieved in Hollywood. . . . The wounded men . . . really look wounded, for almost the first time in a U.S. fiction war film. . . . But by and large the blend of flesh and fantasy is pretty close to Hiltonesque life in the U.S. home.

Joseph Cotten, Jennifer Jones, Shirley Temple, and Claudette Colbert.

Eddie Bracken and Ella Raines having their problems in *Hail the Conquering Hero.*

Hail the Conquering Hero

Paramount

New York release date, August 9, 1944

Produced, directed and written by Preston Sturges.

CAST: Eddie Bracken, Ella Raines, Bill Edwards, Raymond Walburn, William Demarest, Jimmie Dundee, Georgia Caine, Alan Bridge, James Damore, Freddie Steele, Stephen Gregory, Len Hendry, Esther Howard, Elizabeth Patterson, Jimmy Conlin, Arthur Hoyt, Harry Hayden, Franklin Pangborn, Victor Potel, Torben Meyer, Jack Norton, Chester Conklin.

Preston Sturges fashioned an honest, touching home-front comedy-satire about a bewildered youth, played by Eddie Bracken, who is discharged from the Marine Corps because he suffers from hay fever. Bracken then meets William Demarest, a decorated Marine sergeant just returned from Guadalcanal, and his buddies, who decide that the boy should return to his Mom as a medal-bedecked veteran. The fun, for both the audience and Sturges, begins when the boy arrives at home and the whole town turns out to greet him as its "conquering hero" and goes on to nominate him for mayor. His undeserved fame weighs heavily on the lad, however, and, naturally, he ultimately does what any right-thinking American boy would do and confesses the deception—and is rewarded for his honesty.

NEW YORK HERALD TRIBUNE:

... One of the happiest, heartiest film comedies in a twelve-month. . . . Sturges' . . . direction blends well with his script; both are slightly slapstick, but never offensively so. Mob scenes, roughhouses and sharply serious passages are played for all the pantomime they are worth. . . . Bracken again has a chance to display his ability as a comedian. . . . His performance is highly stylized.

Otis L. Guernsey, Jr.

THE NEW YORK TIMES:

Mr. Sturges is just about the sharpest and most rational Hollywood Magi on the job—a fellow with a searching way of looking at the follies of us rather

Eddie Bracken and William Demarest in Preston Sturges' serio-comedy, *Hall the Conquering Hero.*

silly folks . . . this riotously funny motion picture . . . is also one of the wisest ever to burst from a big-time studio.

[Mr. Sturges] is mauling the fetish of the Hero in his latest screen masterpiece. . . . A good· many motion pictures have had bold and penetrating things to say. But Mr. Sturges smiles—nay, laughs—when he says his. Hail the conquering hero, indeed!

Bosley Crowther

NEWSWEEK:

As usual, Sturges has picked his actors where he found them, from familiar players to newcomers like Ella Raines, from old reliables like Raymond Walburn and Franklin Pangborn to reformed stunt men, cinematic has-beens, even prizefighters, and as usual when directed by Sturges, the entire field runs better than form.

Franklin Pangborn, Eddie Bracken, and Ella Raines.

Jane Wyman, Jack Carson, Ann Sheridan, Eve Arden and Alexis Smith in Warner Bros.' comedy, *The Doughgirls*.

The Doughgirls

Warner Bros.

New York release date, August 30, 1944

Produced by Mark Hellinger; directed by James V. Kern; screenplay by Mr. Kern and Sam Hellman; based on the stage play by Joseph A. Fields; additional dialogue by Wilkie Mahoney.

CAST: Ann Sheridan, Alexis Smith, Jack Carson, Jane Wyman, Irene Manning, Charlie Ruggles, Eve Arden, John Ridgely, Alan Mowbray, John Alexander, Craig Stevens, Barbara Brown, Stephen Richards, Francis Pierlot, Donald MacBride, Regis Toomey, Joe De Rita.

The Doughgirls was another comedy centered around the wartime bed shortage in Washington. The hit Broadway play on which it was based concerned a group of unmarried girls, each claiming a husband, settling down in a Washington hotel suite. The Hays office had to be mollified and in the film the play's dialogue and some of the action was rather watered down. But enough of the farce remained to give audiences a good time.

Eve Arden stole the show as a Russian guerrilla in skirts who moves in with the girls, practices her snipership by shooting pigeons from the hotel terrace, and spends much of her time in double features and winds up extricating her roommates from their difficulties.

Alexis Smith had little to do as a lady who finally marries a war hero, and Jane Wyman wasn't very effective as a supposed bride who finds her wedding

Ann Sheridan and Irene Manning.

night interrupted. Ann Sheridan, the film's top-lined star, seemed uncomfortable in the key role of a wise-cracking doughgirl.

NEW YORK HERALD TRIBUNE:
There are several able comic performer at hand to translate the conceit to celluloid, but they are trapped by a clumsy script and inadequate direction. . . . When Ann Sheridan, Jack Carson, Charlie Ruggles and Alan Mowbray are found marking time through one sequence after another, you can be sure that it is no fault of the cast that the picture leaves a great deal to be desired.

Miss Sheridan, who should have been good as the

Charlie Ruggles, Jack Carson, and Jane Wyman.

Jane Wyman, Ann Sheridan, Alexis Smith, chic and sleek as "the doughgirls."

most vocal of the doughgirls, is definitely shaky in this role.

It is the treatment in this Warner Bros. offering which is at fault. . . . James V. Kern, as director and co-adaptor, has let a funny theatrical show elude him on the screen. *The Doughgirls* is rarely funny as it now stands.

Howard Barnes

THE NEW YORK TIMES:

The spectator is required simply to sit there and wonder what's going to turn up next, knowing that the chances are better than even he'll enjoy whatever it happens to be.

. . . On the whole the lines are broad enough and well enough planted to assure the desired reaction. The picture as a whole sets out to make no sense, and it accomplishes that negative aim beautifully and delightfully.

Paul P. Kennedy

Jane Wyman, Alan Mowbray, Alexis Smith, Ann Sheridan in *The Doughgirls*. The film's situations and dialogue were considerably watered down from the stage play.

Skippy Homeier, a Hitler Youth, arrives at his new home in America in in *Tomorrow the World*.

Tomorrow the World

United Artists

New York release date, October 21, 1944

Produced by Lester Cowan; directed by Leslie Fenton; screenplay by Ring Lardner, Jr. and Leopold Atlas; based on the stage play by James Gow and Arnaud D'Usseau.

CAST: Fredric March, Betty Field, Agnes Moorehead, Skippy Homeier, Joan Carroll, Edith Angold, Rudy Wissler, Boots Brown, Marvin Davis, Patsy Ann Thompson, Mary Newton, Tom Fadden.

Skippy Homeier recreated his Broadway role as the twelve-year-old orphaned Hitler youth who finds himself adopted into a family in a "small, average American town." Skippy, a veritable walking hotbed of Nazi ideology, hatreds and prejudices, sets out in a divide-and-conquer fashion to convert everyone he doesn't despise to his National Socialist ways of thinking. Of course he doesn't succeed. Some critics of the day thought that Skippy hadn't made the difficult transition from stage to screen acting successfully and his performance seemed exaggerated. The film did serve to illustrate, however, how the Nazis subverted the minds of children.

NEW YORK HERALD TRIBUNE:

. . . The explosion has been considerably muffled in the film version of the play, now showing at the Globe . . . [its] acid has been diluted for screen presentation; there is very little left of *Tomorrow the World* except the curious oil-and-water mixture of a Nazi among Americans.

Otis L. Guernsey, Jr.

Skippy Homeier and Joan Carroll.

The re-education of Hitler-bred youth to democratic ways of thought and action is indeed a timely and serious subject, one which deserves to be thoughtfully explored on the screen as well as in other media of expression. *Tomorrow the World* is a sincere if not completely satisfying attempt in the right direction. . . . The picture does not convincingly put across its theory that patience, kindness and education in the principles of democracy will do the trick. For it is only after the youthful protagonist is nearly killed and threatened with imprisonment that he displays any inkling of understanding, or appreciating, democracy.

Tomorrow the World can be a very real screen contribution toward the attainment of an enduring peace if it succeeds in impressing upon free minds their responsibility to make certain that no vestige of Nazi ideology will be left smouldering in the Germany of tomorrow.

Thomas M. Pryor

Skippy Homeier confronted by a school principal portrayed by Edith Angold.

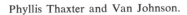
Phyllis Thaxter and Van Johnson.

Thirty Seconds Over Tokyo

MGM

New York release date, November 15, 1944

Produced by Sam Zimbalist; directed by Mervyn LeRoy; screenplay by Dalton Trumbo; based on the book by Captain Ted W. Lawson and Robert Considine.

CAST: Van Johnson, Robert Walker, Phyllis Thaxter, Tim Murdock, Scott McKay, Gordon McDonald, Don DeFore, Robert Mitchum, John R. Reilly, Horace McNally, Donald Curtis, Louis Jean Heydt, Wm. "Bill" Phillips, Douglas Cowan, Paul Langton, Spencer Tracy.

This exciting reconstruction of the famous and heroic air raid on Japan by the men under the command of

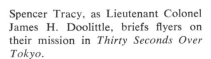
Spencer Tracy, as Lieutenant Colonel James H. Doolittle, briefs flyers on their mission in *Thirty Seconds Over Tokyo.*

Lieutenant Colonel James H. Doolittle (Spencer Tracy here) was based on the best-selling book by Captain Ted Lawson and Bob Considine.

The film, written by Dalton Trumbo and directed by Mervyn LeRoy, had the sharp feel of documentary, calling the raiders by their real-life names and including well-staged and effective battle sequences and aerial photography. It was a blow-by-blow account of the surprise attack, a score-settling for Pearl Harbor, and of the weeks of strenuous and secret preparation that preceded the day when the Army's planes were moved aboard the aircraft carrier *Hornet* in the joint Army-Navy operation.

The scenes dealing with the private life of Capt. Lawson (played by Van Johnson) and his individual exploits vitiated the suspense somewhat, but on the whole, *Thirty Seconds Over Tokyo* was a finely wrought and exciting entertainment, re-creating an important and dramatic episode in the Allied offensive against Japan.

NEWSWEEK:

Accepting the setting of the Swastika as imminent fact, Hollywood now turns out still another propaganda film that is designed to keep the Rising Sun in mind . . . [it is] one of Hollywood's finest war films

Van Johnson and Don DeFore.

to date. . . . Director Mervyn LeRoy achieves sustained drama. . . . As Lawson, Van Johnson comes through with the most effective performance of his career, and Phyllis Thaxter makes her screen debut with an appealing characterization of Lawson's wife.

THE NEW YORK TIMES:

The true and tremendous story of Capt. Ted Lawson and his Army bomber crew, which took part in our first sensational air raid on Japan in April, 1942, is told with magnificent integrity and dramatic eloquence in Metro's film. . . . As the re-created picture of one of our boldest blows in this war and as a drama of personal heroism, it is nigh the best yet made in Hollywood.

. . . All of the production involving planes and technical action is so fine that the film has the tough and literal quality of an Air Force documentary.

It is not in the least surprising that this film was permitted to use the actual names of the principal participants in the "Doolittle raid," for it is a fitting tribute to all of them. And it is certainly a most stimulating and emotionally satisfying film.

Bosley Crowther

NEW YORK HERALD TRIBUNE:

Spencer Tracy plays Doolittle as only he could do it, bringing a cynical but deep emotional power to a part which might have eluded most Hollywood actors.

Howard Barnes

Planes take off from aircraft carrier in
Thirty Seconds Over Tokyo.

Sunday Dinner for a Soldier

20th Century-Fox

New York release date, December 5, 1944

Produced by Walter Morosco; directed by Lloyd Bacon; screenplay by Wanda Tuchock and Melvin Levy; based on a story by Martha Cheavens.

CAST: Anne Baxter, John Hodiak, Charles Winninger, Anne Revere, Connie Marshall, Chill Wills, Robert Bailey, Bobby Driscoll, Jane Darwell, Billy Cummings, Marietta Canty, Barbara Sears, Larry Thompson, Bernie Sell, Chester Conklin.

This was an engaging little film about a poor family, living on a houseboat in Florida, who decide to save and sacrifice in order to invite a lonely soldier for a hopefully sumptuous Sunday meal. The characters

Anne Baxter gets some basic training with a rifle from John Hodiak in *Sunday Dinner for a Soldier*.

Anne Baxter serves John Hodiak Sunday dinner for a soldier.

Charles Winninger, as Gramps, presides over the family meal.

included three small children and their adult (conveniently for the sake of romance) sister, Anne'Baxter, all orphaned and living with their cantankerous old grandfather. John Hodiak was the lucky, hungry GI. The film was popular, unpretentious and effective entertainment.

THE NEW YORKER:

. . . A rather engaging little picture. . . . Anne Baxter, though often obliged to pretend to be dancing to imaginary orchestras, is natural and attractive, and John Hodiak, as the soldier who finally does get his dinner, is very nice, too. . . .

VARIETY:

Sunday Dinner for a Soldier is a modest b.o. film. It's lightweight but has a number of touching moments, particularly for the women.

Hollywood Canteen

Warner Bros.

New York release date, December 15, 1944

Produced by Alex Gottlieb; directed by Delmer Daves; screenplay by Mr. Daves.

CAST: Joan Leslie, Robert Hutton, Dane Clark, Andrews Sisters, Jack Benny, Joe E. Brown, Eddie Cantor, Jack Carson, Joan Crawford, Helmut Dantine, Bette Davis, Faye Emerson, Victor Francen, John Garfield, Sydney Greenstreet, Alan Hale, Paul Henreid, Andrea King, Peter Lorre, Ida Lupino, Irene Manning, Nora Martin, Joan McCracken, Do-
lores Moran, Dennis Morgan, Janis Paige, Eleanor Parker, William Prince, Joyce Reynolds, John Ridgely, Roy Rogers and Trigger, S. Z. Sakall, Zachary Scott, Alexis Smith, Barbara Stanwyck, Craig Stevens, Joseph Szigeti, Donald Woods, Jane Wyman, Jimmy Dorsey and his band, Carmen Cavallaro and orchestra, Golden Gate Quartet, Rosario and Antonio and Sons of the Pioneers.

Warner Bros. had conceived *Hollywood Canteen* as

Joan Leslie and Robert Hutton.

a vehicle documenting what the stars of all the studios were doing for the servicemen who dropped by the Hollywood Canteen. But the other studios declined to "lend" their stars, and the film, as it turned out, seemed to suggest that the Canteen was primarily a Warner Bros. war effort.

Bette Davis, a founder of the Canteen and its president, acted as a sort of mistress of ceremonies for this star-laden entertainment grab-bag in which all the important players under contract at Warner Bros. made guest appearances.

The slim story line presented Robert Hutton and Dane Clark as a couple of soldiers convalescing from wounds suffered in the South Pacific, and Janis Paige and Joan Leslie were the Canteen girls who helped them recover. Their activities—and those of everyone at the Hollywood Canteen—served to bind the picture's many acts together.

Hollywood Canteen was a smash.

VARIETY:

There isn't a marquee big enough to hold all the names in this one, so how can it miss? Besides, it's basically solid. It has story, cohesion and heart. That's not a bad parlay either.

Robert Hutton and Joan Leslie emerge as the real stars of the filmusical. They carry the story, and a

Robert Hutton, Dane Clark, and S.Z. "Cuddles" Sakall in *Hollywood Canteen*. Clark and Hutton portrayed soldiers who wanted to meet movie stars.

Jack Carson, Jane Wyman, John Garfield and Bette Davis sign autographs for a group of avid fans in uniform in *Hollywood Canteen*.

human one it is, too. Miss Leslie plays herself with charm, poise and ease and the plot is so glib one accepts the romance wholeheartedly. . . . In between are interspersed a wealth of specialties, well paced and spaced, so that it doesn't border on the "big short" idea.

NEW YORK POST:

Since *Hollywood Canteen* . . . is the West Coast opposite number of *Stage Door Canteen,* the comparison might as well be made now. *Hollywood Canteen* rivals its predecessor only in size and the number of stars on hand. In story, variety and quality of the acts, the let-down is marked.

Unfortunately the director and author, Delmer Daves, has seen fit to make Corporal Hutton almost a caricature of the Hollywood-worshipping soldier.

There's nothing so good in it that you must attend, just as there is nothing bad enough to keep you away.

Archer Winsten

Victor Francen, Irene Manning, Dane Clark, and Robert Hutton.

Two soldiers, Dane Clark, and Robert Hutton, take it easy while on leave.

Edmond O'Brien, Mark Daniels, Barry Nelson, and Gary Merrill await word on a missing plane.

Winged Victory

20th Century-Fox

New York release date, December 20, 1944

Produced by Darryl F. Zanuck; directed by George Cukor; stage and screen play by Moss Hart.

CAST: Pvt. Lon McCallister, Jeanne Crain, Sgt. Edmond O'Brien, Jane Ball, Sgt. Mark Daniels, Jo-Carroll Dennison, Cpl. Don Taylor, Judy Holliday, Cpl. Lee J. Cobb, T/Sgt. Peter Lind Hayes, Cpl. Alan Baxter, Geraldine Wall, Cpl. Red Buttons, Cpl. Barry Nelson, Sgt. Rune Hultman, Cpl. Gary Merrill, Sgt. George Reeves, Pfc. George Petrie, Pfc. Alfred Ryder, Cpl. Karl Malden, Pfc. Martin Ritt, Cpl. Harry Lewis, Corp. Henry Rowland, S/Sgt. Sascha Brastoff, Cpl. Archie Robbins, Cpl. Jack Slate, Pfc. Henry Slate.

Darryl Zanuck's tribute to the Army Air Corps pilot-training program hewed closely to the Moss Hart play on which it was based. Directed by George Cukor, the film, whose profits went to Army charities, began with a title card announcing "All men appearing in uniform are members of the armed services." The film was also made with the full cooperation of

Barry Nelson, Jeanne Crain, Judy Holliday, Edmond O'Brien, Jo-Carroll Dennison, Mark Daniels, Don Taylor in *Winged Victory*.

Judy Holliday, Jeanne Crain, and Jo-Carroll Dennison.

the Air Corps, which allowed the use of hundreds of uniformed extras in several marching-and-singing scenes. In fact, it often seemed that the Army Air Corps Chorus was hovering around every corner, since ten minutes seldom elapsed without the men bursting into patriotic song, either on screen or off.

The film was at its best when it stuck to the train-ing and testing of potential pilots, but it turned to pure sentimentalized corn—with matching banal dia-logue—when it dealt with the personal romantic in-volvements of its principals, played by Lon McCal-lister, Edmond O'Brien, Mark Daniels, Don Taylor and Barry Nelson.

There were several very effective scenes, including

Edmond O'Brien, Don Taylor, and fellow airmen share a light moment.

Judy Holliday and Jeanne Crain, as airmen's wives, share their anxieties in *Winged Victory*.

Don Taylor and fellow flyers in an animated discussion.

one near the end of the picture with three pilots' wives—Judy Holliday, Jeanne Crain and Jo-Carroll Dennison—who watch from a hotel room as their husbands' planes take off in the San Francisco dawn and head out over the Golden Gate for the Pacific and combat.

Winged Victory was, on the whole, an honest, informative film, but one lacking dramatic strength and emotional appeal.

TIME:

Moss Hart's crisply flamboyant salute to the Air Forces . . . would gain considerably if it did not so

often suggest a Boy Scout Jamboree. . . . The best parts of *Winged Victory* are less like drama than like document, except that documentary films are seldom half as well-made or a tenth as enjoyable.

THE NEW YORK TIMES:

. . . It gives every promise of being one of the most successful films about this war. . . . There is no question that Mr. Hart captured much of the gallantry and pathos of youth rushing toward dangerous adventures with surface enthusiasm and inner dread.

Bosley Crowther

Edmond O'Brien meets Mark Daniels as he arrives for training.

The poster for *Objective Burma!* featured Errol Flynn in a determined pose that should have given any hostile Japanese pause.

Objective Burma

Warner Bros.

New York release date, January 26, 1945

Produced by Jerry Wald; directed by Raoul Walsh; screenplay by Ranald MacDougall and Lester Cole; based on a story by Alvah Bessie.

CAST: Errol Flynn, William Prince, James Brown, George Tobias, Henry Hull, Warner Anderson, John Alvin, Stephen Richards, Dick Erdman, Tony Caruso, Hugh Beaumont, John Whitney, Joel Allen, Buddy Yarus, Frank Tang, William Hudson, Rodric Red Wing, Asit Koomar, John Sheridan, Lester Matthews.

Objective Burma was a grittily "realistic" study of men in war. Errol Flynn starred as Captain Nelson, commander of a fifty-man unit of paratroopers who

Errol Flynn led the mission in *Objective Burma!*

George Tobias and James Brown.

are dropped 180 miles behind enemy lines to blow up a strategic radar station that is the key factor in Japanese occupiers' defense of Burma.

After Flynn's men have accomplished their mission without much difficulty, they rendezvous to await an airlift to safety. But when the planes arrive, they cannot land because a Jap force suddenly attacks. Flynn and his fighters must then seek an alternate way out of the Burmese jungles. The alternative involves fighting their way through 150 miles of enemy-infested jungle. Of the fifty men who set out only a dozen survive, but as they make a last-ditch effort to defend the hill where they have been surrounded, the sky is suddenly filled with wave after wave of bombers and paratroopers signalling the Allied offensive that freed Burma.

Objective Burma was criticized by some British because, according to them, it gave the impression

218

that Errol Flynn, an American, had routed the Japanese from Burma singlehandedly, while in reality the operation was a joint British-American one.

THE NEW YORK TIMES:

The Warners have achieved a startling degree of realism. . . . This is without question one of the best war films yet made in Hollywood. There are no phony heroics by Errol Flynn or any of the other members of a uniformly excellent cast. . . .

Thomas M. Pryor

TIME:

. . . A tribute to the U.S. paratroops. At the rate Errol Flynn & Co. knock off the Japanese, it may make you wonder why there is any good reason for the war to outlast next weekend. . . .

This story is used not as an excuse for histrionic heroics but as a basis for a good deal of dogged, specific detail about men at war. . . .

Objective Burma gets pretty long and you can seldom forget that its soldiers are really just actors; but within the limits possible to fictional war movies, it is about as good as they come.

Warner Anderson, Hugh Beaumont and Stephen Richards (who later changed his name to Mark Stevens).

God Is My Co-Pilot

Warner Bros.

New York release date, March 23, 1945

Produced by Robert Buckner; directed by Robert Florey; screenplay by Peter Milne; based on the book by Col. Robert L. Scott.

CAST: Dennis Morgan, Dane Clark, Raymond Massey, Alan Hale, Andrea King, John Ridgely, Stanley Ridges, Craig Stevens, Warren Douglas, Stephen Richards, Charles Smith, Minor Watson, Richard Loo.

Warner Bros.' screen adaptation of the best-selling book by Colonel Robert Lee Scott re-created the story of the 34-year-old Georgia flyer who refused to accept the Army's notion that he was too old for aerial warfare and became a hero with General Claire Chennault's "Flying Tigers."

After participating in the bombing of Hong Kong, Scott was forced down in enemy territory, but survived and returned to teach other Army airmen what he had learned during his ordeal in China.

Dennis Morgan played Col. Scott with sincerity, but the religious undertones, Warner Bros.-style, de-

Raymond Massey and Dennis Morgan.

Alan Hale and other Japanese prisoners of war in *God Is My Co-Pilot*.

tracted from the overall effectiveness and excitement of the picture, which became dull during its stretches on the ground. At times the spiritualism was a little beyond the bounds of credibility.

THE NEW YORK TIMES:
Obviously Warner Bros. took the title of Col. Robert L. Scott's war book, *God Is My Co-Pilot,* much more literally than the author did. For their rip-roaring film . . . is heavily—and often embarrassingly—larded with piety. . . . For Colonel Scott's popular, vivid story of his career as a fighter-pilot in the Far East has been turned by the Warners into another rather cheaply theatrical war film.

Bosley Crowther

Raymond Massey, Dennis Morgan, and Dane Clark.

NEW YORK HERALD TRIBUNE:

... A slapped together attraction. ... When *God Is My Co-Pilot* is not upstairs, as aviation lingo has it, it is about as trite and unconvincing as any war film that you may cite. For all the flashbacks, supposedly emotional scenes and fragments of philosophy which punctuate the aerial action vitiate a tale which might have been a notable addition to the screen's extensive considerations of the far-flung theatres of the war.

Howard Barnes

NEWSWEEK:

When *God Is My Co-Pilot* takes to the wild blue yonder, it is a reasonably exciting story of air war over China. Aground, unfortunately, the Warner production is just another service film. ... It bears the unmistakable stamp of truth. Yet, despite individual and group heroism, the film treatment is perfunctory and uninspired.

Dennis Morgan strafes a column of Japanese soldiers.

The German Army surrendered to the Allies on May 7, 1945 and the war in Europe was over.

Blood on the Sun

United Artists

New York release date, June 28, 1945

Produced by William Cagney; directed by Frank Lloyd; screenplay by Lester Cole; based on a story by Garrett Fort.

CAST: James Cagney, Sylvia Sidney, Wallace Ford, Rosemary De Camp, Robert Armstrong, John Emery, Leonard Strong, Frank Puglia, Jack Halloran, Hugh Ho, Philip Ahn, Joseph Kim, Marvin Mueller, Rhys Williams, Porter Hall, James Bell, Grace Lem, Oy Chan, George Paris, Hugh Beaumont.

James Cagney starred as an American newspaper writer for *The Tokyo Chronicle* in Tokyo circa 1929 in a pure fiction intrigue melodrama revolving around Cagney's efforts to hold on to and smuggle out of the country the secret Tanaka plan for Japanese world conquest.

Cagney was assisted in his heroics by Sylvia Sidney,

Leonard Strong and Jack Sergel as Imperial Secret Police in *Blood on the Sun.*

Sylvia Sidney in the clutches of evil Baron Tanaka (John Emery).

James Cagney and Sylvia Sidney receive the "Tanaka Plan."

in her first screen appearance since 1941, as an attractive Anglo-Chinese double agent who has a score to settle with the Japanese.

The attempt to weave the very real historical document into the fictions of the film's plot tended to undermine its believability, but Cagney provided enough derring-do, fist-swinging and Judo (beating a hulking Jap at his own game) to keep up the interest. Without his performance, however, it would have been a rather routine business.

THE NEW YORK TIMES:

The thesis that one good American can lick any number of Japs doing anything from using the old think-box to fighting in the native Judy style is expounded with considerable cocksureness and magni-

James Cagney is visited by Jack Halloran, a Japanese secret police officer.

ficent muscular display in James Cagney's latest picture.

. . . We have here an entertaining movie in the time-honored Cagney groove—tough, hard-hitting and explosive, with just enough rudimentary suspense. But let's not approve it too quickly; it treads too boldly upon critical ground. In the first place, it makes a pulpwood fiction out of a historic incident. And more than that, it puts the Japs in the popular but highly deceptive "monkey" class. A true comprehension of our enemies and the sort of people with whom we'll later have to cope is brusquely waylaid by a picture as glibly cocky as *Blood on the Sun*.

Bosley Crowther

NEW YORK HERALD TRIBUNE:

Pure, unadulterated melodrama has a safe niche in cinematic offerings, but this fol-de-rol is more pretentious than persuasive. . . .

Howard Barnes

NEWSWEEK:

. . . It is typical of this film that, when the embattled American is finally overwhelmed by Tokyo's best snipers and gumshoe men, he is still able to stagger gallantly to his feet and hobble off to the safety of the American Embassy. Obviously nothing would be gained for the studio by killing off a guy who had licked considerably more than his weight in wild Japs—and had Miss Sidney waiting for him in China.

TIME:

. . . Liberal Actor-Producer Cagney is a man of sense and good will. He takes care, even in the midst of this angry bit of patriotism, to show that there are honorable and anti-militaristic Japanese as well as the sort who took the nation over—and that there have been treacherous Americans. As notably, he develops serious intentions towards a Eurasian girl, coolly counters her it-can-never-be demurrers with: "That's an insult to the Irish."

Eleanor Parker and John Garfield in *Pride of the Marines.*

Pride of the Marines

Warner Bros.

New York releae date, August 24, 1945

Produced by Jerry Wald; directed by Delmer Daves; screenplay by Albert Maltz; adaptation by Marvin Borowsky from a book by Roger Butterfield.

CAST: John Garfield, Eleanor Parker, Dane Clark, John Ridgely, Rosemary De Camp, Ann Doran, Ann Todd, Warren Douglas, Don McGuire, Tom D'Andrea, Rory Mallinson, Stephen Richards, Anthony Caruso, Moroni Olsen, Dave Willock, John Sheridan, John Miles, John Compton, Lennie Bremen, Michael Brown.

This highly pertinent film was based on the true story of Al Schmid, a young Marine who lost his eyesight during the battle of Guadalcanal. It was also the tough tale of an average American youngster and his girl friend who fought the war on different fronts with immense courage. Done in a semi-documentary

John Garfield as real-life Marine Al Schmid.

John Garfield, Anthony Caruso, and Dane Clark.

Rory Mallinson, Rosemary DeCamp, and John Garfield.

style, the picture movingly recounted the long and difficult struggle of a hero who has to recover his nerve for the battle of going through life as a blind man.

Screenwriter Albert Maltz, later to be one of Hollywood's "blacklisted," was accused by some of injecting too much "social consciousness" into the segments dealing with Schmid's working class origin and early life; nevertheless, the film was extremely topical. Preceding *The Best Years of Our Lives,* it attempted to help returning veterans, especially the handicapped, and their families to adjust to postwar conditions. Ironically, the ads for the film pictured stars John Garfield, Eleanor Parker and Dane Clark walking arm-in-arm and smiling broadly, as if in an MGM musical comedy instead of a serious social drama.

TIME:

. . . Hollywood's most serious attempt yet to picture some of the problems of returning servicemen. . . .

Even when it drags, the screen story of Al Schmid

has a compelling doggedness and honesty. The cast, especially Messrs. Garfield and Clark, put it over with a notable absence of affectation. . . .

It is also exciting—because the screen is so unaccustomed to plain talk—to see and hear the angry discussion of postwar prospects which Scripter Albert Maltz has written for the hospitalized marines. . . .

NEW YORK HERALD TRIBUNE:

Although the war scenes are about the finest that have appeared in a Hollywood production, there is a sensitive probing of human experience in most of the sequences which gives the work a certain timeless quality. . . . Thanks to John Garfield's brilliant portrayal of the central role, Schmid emerges on the screen with genuine personal authority. Thanks to a remarkably realistic treatment, the motion picture has over-all conviction.

Garfield's under-acting keys the production to its central theme, but Eleanor Parker lends invaluable support as the girl Schmid leaves behind him in Philadelphia who wants him back, blind or not. . . .

Howard Barnes

John Garfield.

Moroni Olsen, Dane Clark, Rosemary DeCamp and John Garfield. Schmid has to adjust to his blindness.

By September 2, 1945 World War II
was officially over.

The House on Ninety-Second Street

20th Century-Fox

New York release date, September 26, 1945

Produced by Louis de Rochemont; directed by Henry
Hathaway; screenplay by Charles G. Booth; based
on a story by Mr. Booth taken from cases in Federal
Bureau of Investigation files.

CAST: William Eythe, Lloyd Nolan, Signe Hasso,
Gene Lockhart, Leo G. Carroll, Lydia St. Clair, Wil-
liam Post, Jr., Harry Bellaver, Bruno Wick, Harro
Meller, Charles Wagenheim, Alfred Linder, Renee
Carson, Rusty Lane, John McKee, Edwin Jerome,
Elisabeth Neumann, Salo Douday, Paul Ford, Wil-
liam Adams, Lew Eckles, Tom Brown, George Shel-
ton, Alfred Ziesler.

Producer Louis de Rochemont's twenty-two years of
newsreel and documentary experience, combined with
material from the files of the FBI and actual film
footage shot by G-men, served to bring a great deal
of power and excitement to this quasi-documentary
about Nazi spies in America and the G-men on their
trails.

William Eythe with Nazi spies in *The House on 92nd Street.*

Lloyd Nolan confronts Nazi spy Gene Lockhart.

The realistic look of the film was enhanced by the use of some of the actual locations in New York City and on Long Island where the real enemy agents had worked and carried out their espionage activities. This "realism" was further heightened by the casting of unfamiliar actors as the spies and counter-spies and the use of real federal agents in some of the roles.

The film was extremely timely, so much so that it was updated after completion. When it was released, there was a foreword explaining that the "process 97" Nazi agents were trying to steal was actually a part of the atomic bomb formula. The development of the super-bomb had, of course, been top secret until its use on Hiroshima and Nagasaki only a few weeks before the film's release.

The House on Ninety-Second Street was a re-

Signe Hasso introduces William Eythe to her fellow Nazi agents.

Leo G. Carroll and Signe Hasso question William Eythe when they find out he is working for the FBI.

markable demonstration of Hollywood's ability to wrest exciting screen drama directly from the headlines of the day.

THE NEW YORK TIMES:

Louis de Rochemont, the producer, and his director, Henry Hathaway, have achieved a most successful blending of the documentary and conventional techniques, thus proving that realism can be entertaining,

too. . . . The FBI agents, other than Mr. Nolan, are genuine and his performance is so restrained and unimposing in a theatrical sense that one accepts his inspector Briggs as being the real thing. . . . As the ring leader of the spies, Miss Hasso tends to be over-domineering at times, but the other enemy agents of assorted wiliness are excellently drawn by Leo G. Carroll, Lydia St. Clair, Harry Bellaver, Conrad Arbulf and Alfred Linder.

Thomas M. Pryor

TIME:

. . . How J. Edgar Hoover's G-men saved the day is the tense story of *The House on Ninety-Second Street*. The desperate goings-on centering around an inconspicuous Manhattan brownstone building . . . escape the routine of cloak-and-dagger melodrama by their realism. . . .

The de Rochemont-Hathaway-Monks approach to a purely fictional drama somehow suggests that the people on the screen are real and just happen to have been caught by fortuitous camera. Actually, some of the film's G-men are the real McCoy. The picture serves up, as an added fillip, real FBI shots of a pre-Pearl Harbor traffic in and out of the German Embassy.

For those who believe that naive Americans are no match for wily Europeans in the spy trade, and for those who just like their movies to move, "The House" is recommended entertainment.

Lloyd Nolan playing FBI investigator.

Robert Mitchum.

The Story of G.I. Joe

United Artists

New York release date, October 5, 1945

Produced by Lester Cowan; directed by William A. Wellman; screenplay by Leopold Atlas, Guy Endore and Philip Stevenson.

CAST: Burgess Meredith, Robert Mitchum, Freddie Steele, Wally Cassell, Jimmy Lloyd, Jack Reilly, Bill Murphy.

William Wellman directed this film almost as if he were making a documentary, skipping false and manufactured heroics to concentrate on facts. Basically the theme of the picture was that an infantryman lives miserably and dies miserably.

The film, inspired by war correspondent Ernie Pyle (played on screen by Burgess Meredith), was an honest tribute to the footsoldier and a tough record of stubborn fighting, illuminating the curious paradox of a peace-loving democracy fighting with the spirit of a warrior nation. Much of the authenticity of *Story of G.I. Joe* was achieved through the use of Army film clips taken during actual battles.

Burgess Meredith portrayed correspondent Ernie Pyle in Story of G.I. Joe.

THE NEW YORK TIMES:

The little men from a thousand different walks of life who were swept in the whirlpool of international

Burgess Meredith.

discord to the battlefields of Europe and the Pacific ... are projected in all their true glory in [this] eloquent motion picture ... a hard-hitting, penetrating drama of the footslogging soldier. ...

... The scenarists, the director and the players have animated Mr. Pyle's chronicles in a manner that is truly inspired. ...

It is humorous, poignant and tragic, an earnestly human reflection of a stern life and the dignity of man. ... Director William Wellman's approach is starkly realistic. ...

When the men of the Fifth Army, many of whom participate in the picture, saw *Story of G.I. Joe* in Italy, their verdict was "This is it!"

Thomas M. Pryor

TIME:

... An attempt to picture the infantryman's war as the late Ernie Pyle saw it. Pyle himself and nine fellow correspondents supervised and vouched for the movie's hard-bitten authenticity. The result is far and away the least glamorous war picture ever made. It is a movie without a single false note. It is not "entertainment" in the usual sense, but General Eisenhower called it "the greatest war picture I've ever seen."

NEW YORK HERALD TRIBUNE:

... Burgess Meredith plays the late fox-hole reporter with tremendous power and restraint. ...

... The tale of men who live and fight together, wanting nothing more than to be back home again, is integrated in a savage and dynamic unity. ... It is at once a reminder of the things that these men fought and died for recently, and that these things are the core of democracy.

Howard Barnes

Burgess Meredith.

233

John Wayne and Donna Reed.

They Were Expendable

MGM

New York release date, December 20, 1945

Produced and directed by John Ford; screenplay by Frank Wead; based on the book by William L. White.

CAST: Robert Montgomery, John Wayne, Donna Reed, Jack Holt, Ward Bond, Marshall Thompson, Paul Langton, Leon Ames, Arthur Walsh, Donald Curtis, Cameron Mitchell, Jeff York, Murray Alper, Harry Tenbrook, Jack Pennick, Alex Havier, Charles Trowbridge, Robert Barrat, Bruce Kellogg, Tim Murdock, Louis Jean Heydt, Russell Simpson, Vernon Steele.

"In a war, anything can be expendable—money or gasoline or equipment or, most usually, men." So a young Naval lieutenant told William L. White, whose 1942 best-seller was the basis for John Ford's film about the men who manned the little motor torpedo boats during the desperate days in the Philippines when the Japanese fleet had little other opposition.

Robert Montgomery, only recently returned from fighting in the Pacific, starred as the commander of the squadron fighting a delaying action against the enemy. John Wayne was also on hand as a captain of one of the boats. The emphasis throughout was on action, and dialogue was kept to a minimum.

Director Ford was himself a Navy veteran and his film was an abiding testament to the valor that made ultimate victory possible.

NEWSWEEK:

Although Hollywood is a little late in releasing its version of William L. White's best seller, *They Were Expendable,* the timing is irrelevant. This is one of the fine war movies and a stirring reminder of American gallantry in the early days of disaster.

The acting is first-rate throughout, but the film is at its documentary best in action, whether the sea-going gadflies are nipping at a Kuma-class cruiser or, in the blackest day of the campaign, whisking General MacArthur to his historic rendezvous off Mindanao. . . .

TIME:

In trying to steer between war melodrama and straight

Ward Bond and Robert Montgomery in *They Were Expendable*.

documentary reporting, "Expendable" beats a middle course through waters that are too rough for speed.

NEW YORK HERALD TRIBUNE:
There has been a notion around that war pictures were dated. The Messrs. Ford and Montgomery give it the lie.... Ford... has framed sequence after sequence with such consummate skill and knowledge that one is given a key to recent conflict as well as a fiercely moving account of that conflict.

[*They Were Expendable*] is way up in the top brackets of movie making.... The actors have obviously had something to do with this. Montgomery is especially striking as the commander of the expendable little squadron.... He plays with a quiet authority which always defines a scene in its human aspects. John Wayne is excellent as another skipper and so are too many performers to list here.... *They Were Expendable* is a memorable war film.

Howard Barnes

Robert Montgomery and John Wayne.

235

A Walk in the Sun

20th Century-Fox

New York release date, January 11, 1946

Produced and directed by Lewis Milestone; screenplay by Robert Rossen; based on the novel by Harry Brown.

CAST: Dana Andrews, Richard Conte, Sterling Holloway, George Tyne, John Ireland, Herbert Rudley, Richard Benedict, Norman Lloyd, Lloyd Bridges, Huntz Hall, James Cardwell, Chris Drake, George Offerman, Jr., Danny Desmond, Victor Cutler, Steve Brodie, Al Hammer, Matt Willis, Anthony Dante, Robert Lowell.

A Walk in the Sun dealt with a small battle in the big war and with the importance of such confrontations in relation to the larger conflict.

In narrowing its scope to one small but excruciating action—the attempt to overcome a Nazi stronghold a few miles inland of an Italian beachhead—the movie hit the core of what must have actually happened in countless small encounters on battlefields wherever American fighting men met the enemy.

Screenwriter Robert Rossen's and director Lewis Milestone's film concerned itself intimately and in

Dana Andrews, Lloyd Bridges, John Ireland in
A Walk in the Sun.

Lewis Milestone directed Richard Conte, Dana Andrews, Lloyd Bridges.

close-up with the men involved, with their thoughts and feelings. It was a compelling and honest account of humans caught in the mill of an inhuman situation.

NEW YORK HERALD TRIBUNE:

Robert Rossen has converted the Harry Brown novel to screen coinage with something of an alchemist's skill. And an all-male cast gives the story of a platoon ... the surging tragedy and triumph which it deserved. ... [This] is a motion picture epic of embattled democracy. ...

Of all our top directors [Milestone] is the one who knows best how to couple imagery and dialogue in a fascinating film fugue. The camera always accents the insistent and terrible sequences of a minor maneuver. ...

Dana Andrews has the chief role of Sergeant Tyne and plays it with the quiet intensity one might have expected from a knowing actor. ...

Howard Barnes

NEWSWEEK:

Ex-Pvt. Harry Brown's best-seller was one of the few fine novels to come out of the war; it loses none of its honesty and distinction in going Hollywood. ...

Milestone, who knows what to do with a war movie, misses no chance for action or accumulative suspense. ...

Steve Brodie and Richard Conte.

On a Salerno beachhead.

Orson Welles and Loretta Young.

The Stranger

RKO

New York release date, July 10, 1946

Produced by S. P. Eagle for International Pictures; directed by Orson Welles; screenplay by Anthony Veiller; based on a story by Victor Trivas and Decla Dunning.

CAST: Edward G. Robinson, Loretta Young, Orson Welles, Philip Merivale, Billy House, Richard Long, Konstantin Shayne, Martha Wentworth, Byron Deith, Pietro Sosso.

Orson Welles directed and starred in this chilling film that suggested that the world had not heard the last from German fascism. Welles portrayed a top Nazi, one of the architects of the concentration death camps, hiding out from the Allied War Crimes Com-

mission by posing as a mild-mannered prep-school professor in a quiet little New England town.

Not even Welles' pretty young screen wife, Loretta Young, knew of his evil past. But Welles was plotting new Nazi terror even as G-man Edward G. Robinson closed in.

The film built up suspense as audiences wondered whether the unsuspecting Loretta would become Welles' murder victim before he was caught and brought to justice.

THE NEW YORK TIMES:

Orson Welles plainly gets much pleasure out of playing villainous roles . . . in this custom-made melodrama . . . he is playing the role of the big-brain behind the Nazi torture camps. . . . Only—this is the

Orson Welles and Loretta Young.

crux of the story—all that is behind him now, and he is living successfully incognito in a little Connecticut town. . . .

. . . The performance of Mr. Welles in the title role is one of the less convincing features of this film . . . the writing . . . is the weakest thing about it. . . .

. . . Edward G. Robinson is well restrained as the unrelenting sleuth. . . . But the whole film . . . comes off a bloodless, manufactured show. The atom-bomb newsreels on the same bill are immeasurably more frightening.

Bosley Crowther

TIME:

All of the acting is well above par. . . . And Actor Welles, even though Director Welles has used too much film on shots of the petulant Welles scowl, is a convincing menace who richly deserves hissing.

Orson Welles at his malevolent best in *The Stranger* with Loretta Young as his endangered wife.

Sylvia Sidney.

The Searching Wind

Paramount

New York release date, June 26, 1946

Produced by Hal Wallis; directed by William Dieterle; screenplay by Lillian Hellman based on her play.

CAST: Robert Young, Sylvia Sidney, Ann Richards, Dudley Digges, Albert Basserman, Dan Seymour, Ian Wolfe, Marietta Canty, Norma Varden, Charles D. Brown, Don Castle, William Trenk, Mickey Kuhn, Ann Carter, Dave Willock, Douglas Dick.

This film is noteworthy since it was released so soon after the war's end and although it dealt with a family's problems and a love triangle there were some brilliant moments of philosophy about war and its absurdity.

Douglas Dick plays the son who recently returned from the war and is about to have his leg amputated. He gives a marvelous speech foretelling that the youth of America is going to be shocked to learn that what they fought for, gave their limbs for, is going to prove to be worthless.

Albert Basserman also has a marvelous bit as an old-line Prussian diplomat who philosophically views the Nazis and quietly retires to Switzerland at the time of the Munich appeasement.

Although the theme of the film was timely and important the story bogged down and most reviews were mixed.

240

NEW YORK HERALD TRIBUNE:

The story pits three generations of solid Americans against each other, as they try to understand the horror that happened on the face of the earth in the space of forty years. The grandfather preferred retirement . . . his daughter and son-in-law played politics . . . hoping they were doing their best. The kid . . . got his leg shot to pieces . . . and questioned the wisdom of his elders. . . . Robert Young makes a laudable, if rather feeble, effort to personify American isolationism during two decades.

Howard Barnes

THE NEW YORK TIMES:

On the strength of its best intention, which evidently is to expose the peril of leaving worldwide problems to the striped-pants diplomats, the most respectful approval must be given *The Searching Wind*.

. . . The structure of the drama is weak and the playwright apparently was unable to view her villains with convincing contempt. Indeed, the estimations of the weaklings in this film are so washed with pleasantries and romance that they attract more sympathy than hate. . . . This tale might have made for gripping drama if clearly and angrily told in terms of sharp personal conflict such as Miss Hellman employed in *Watch on the Rhine*. But regrettably, the rifts among the characters—as well as the conflicts within themselves—are very fuzzy and inconclusive.

Ann Richards and Robert Young.

The issues are never boldly drawn. And, despite a great deal of conversation, no one ever states his case in trenchant words—not even the son who, at the finish, makes a plea for brave and square diplomacy.

Bosley Crowther

Reginald Sheffield as "the prissy little man."

Gary Cooper and Lilli Palmer.

Cloak and Dagger

Warner Bros.

New York release date, October 4, 1946

Produced by Milton Sperling; directed by Fritz Lang; screenplay by Albert Maltz and Ring Lardner, Jr.; based on an original story by Boris Ingster and John Larkin; suggested by the book by Corey Ford and Alastair McBain.

CAST: Gary Cooper, Lilli Palmer, Robert Alda, Vladimir Sokoloff, J. Edward Bromberg, Marjorie Hoshelle, Ludwig Stossel, Helen Thimig, Dan Seymour, Marc Lawrence, James Flavin.

This film is significant because of its attitude and treatment of the subject of nuclear weapons. Although the film, as released, eventually turns into melodramatic slush, there is a great sequence at the beginning. Gary Cooper portrays a college professor,

a nuclear physicist, from a Midwestern University. When he is approached by the OSS to aid them in learning how far the Nazis have progressed with their atomic energy research he gives an impassioned speech stating that at last the world community of scientists has been banded together toward one goal. But is that goal a search for a cancer cure? Is that goal to aid mankind in its fight against the diseases and hardships of life? No. The goal is to create the greatest destructive force known to man.

Cooper's inspired monologue about the use and possible misuse of atomic energy is totally out of key with the rest of the film—undoubtedly because Warner Bros. would not let director Fritz Lang release the film he had shot.

In the version seen by the public the film ends with Cooper completing his mission, rescuing the Italian scientist and accompanying him back to the Allies. He leaves Lilli Palmer behind but it is implied he will return for her after the war. Director Lang has said that in the original ending the scientist dies on the plane and the British and U.S. secret service men must further pursue the Nazis. From a photo left by the scientist they surmise that the Nazis have an installation in Bavaria. They find the site has been abandoned and there is dialogue to this effect: "Probably the plant is in Argentina now—or somewhere."

Lang has stated that the final fadeout had Cooper walking out of the abandoned cave seeing an American soldier. The sun is shining, birds are singing and Cooper says, "This is the Year One of the Atomic Age and God help us if we think we can keep this secret from the world, and keep it for ourselves."

According to the director the entire fourth reel was cut and probably doesn't exist any longer. He assumes that Warners cut his ending because it was too soon after bombs had been dropped on Hiroshima and Nagasaki.

NEWSWEEK:

Cloak and Dagger is just a "B" plot dressed up in "A" trimmings. . . . Cooper doesn't seem particularly happy in his role, and even such an expert director as Fritz Lang has trouble whipping up dollops of violent action to create the illusion of suspense. . . . Fortunately, the love interest is refreshingly represented by Lilli Palmer, an English screen star whose American debut entitles her to stay in Hollywood as long as she likes.

THE NEW YORK TIMES:

When someone invented the nickname, "the cloak and dagger boys," for the daring intelligence officers of the wartime OSS, that someone was being ironic in a grimly humorous way and throwing a bit of sarcasm in the direction of Hollywood, for some of the missions of those agents had a marked cinematic flair. Only, of course, there were manifest points of difference. That's what made it a joke.

However, the people in Hollywood have missed the irony and have gladly embraced the opportunity to take over the OSS . . . [this] is a straight "cloak and dagger" film, with all of the elements of adventure and romance that the classification implies. Apart from the realm of realities, it is fast entertainment on the screen. . . .

Bosley Crowther

J. Edward Bromberg and Gary Cooper as secret agents in *Cloak and Dagger*.

243

The Best Years of Our Lives

RKO

New York release date, November 21, 1946

Produced by Samuel Goldwyn; directed by William Wyler; screenplay by Robert E. Sherwood; based on a novel by MacKinlay Kantor.

·CAST: Myrna Loy, Fredric March, Dana Andrews, Teresa Wright, Virginia Mayo, Cathy O'Donnell, Hoagy Carmichael, Harold Russell, Gladys George, Roman Bohnen, Ray Collins, Steve Cochran, Minna Gombell, Walter Baldwin, Dorothy Adams.

A *Time* magazine photo and story of homeward-bound G.I.'s allegedly gave Samuel Goldwyn the idea for *The Best Years of Our Lives.* Goldwyn spotted the article, phoned novelist MacKinlay Kantor and asked him for a story treatment which became the basis for Kantor's novel, *Glory for Me,* from which Robert E. Sherwood wrote the script. Director William Wyler was particularly interested in making the film about the problems returning vets faced, since he had spent three and a half years in the Air Force and had had his own problems with reconverting to civilian life.

The picture, with a fictional "average middle-American city as its backdrop, dealt with postwar readjustment and reconversion problems in intensely human and dramatically compelling terms. It told of the return home of three veterans: a banker (Fredric March) who had become a sergeant; a soda jerk (Dana Andrews) who was a decorated Air Corps captain; and a high school kid (Harold Russell) who lost both hands in service with the Navy. Each of these characters was realistic and honest enough to have stood alone, but their stories and lives were skillfully interwoven into a moving and coherent whole.

The romantic and happy ending of *The Best Years of Our Lives* had the amputee finding the courage to marry his childhood sweetheart and the hero from the drugstore making an implicit romantic pact with the daughter of the banker. It was easily a message of hope and continuation for a nation still suffering the wounds of war.

The Best Years of our Lives received Academy Awards for Best Picture, Best Actor (Fredric

Cathy O'Donnell and Harold Russell.

March), Best Supporting Actor (Harold Russell), Best Direction (William Wyler), Best Screenplay (Robert E. Sherwood), Best Editing and Best Music Score. In addition, Harold Russell received a special award "for bringing hope and courage to his fellow veterans through his appearance in *The Best Years of Our Lives.*"

THE NEW YORK TIMES:

It is seldom that there comes a motion picture which can be wholly and enthusiastically endorsed not only as superlative entertainment but as food for quiet and humanizing thought. Yet such a one . . . is *The Best Years of Our Lives.* . . . Cut, as it were, from the heart-wood of contemporary American life, this film . . . gives off a warm glow of affection for everyday, down-to-earth folks.

. . . [This film] catches the drama of veterans returning home from war as no film—or play or novel that we've yet heard of—has managed to do. . . . It fully reflects the delicate tensions, the deep anxieties and the gnawing despairs that surely have been experienced by most such fellows who have been through the same routine. . . .

Myrna Loy and Fredric March readjust to each other in *The Best Years of Our Lives.*

Teresa Wright and Dana Andrews.

Myrna Loy, Fredric March, and
Teresa Wright.

...In working out their solutions Mr. Sherwood and Mr. Wyler have achieved some of the most beautiful and inspiring demonstrations of human fortitude that we have had in films....

Bosley Crowther

NEW YORK HERALD TRIBUNE:
The screen unleashes a full measure of its latent power and wonder.... Rarely have the potentialities of a medium been so dazzlingly disclosed as they are. ... The result is a work of provocative and moving insistence and beauty. William Wyler has staged it with superb detachment and skill. Fredric March, Teresa Wright, Dana Andrews, Myrna Loy and the other players interpret it with unerring understanding.

Howard Barnes

TIME:
Most notable performance (and the one which best shows off Director Wyler's skill) is given by ex-Paratrooper Harold Russell, 32. Cast as a handicapped sailor named Homer Parish, Russell actually plays himself. He is no actor and no one pretends that he is, but his performance is more affecting than any professional's could be. Director Wyler merely surrounded Russell with plot and let the cameraman follow the calm, strong, unhandsome Russell face. The audience fills in all the emotion that is needed as the unembarrassed camera studies the two skillfully articulated metal hooks that Russell has learned to use in place of the hands that were blown off on D-day.

The Aftermath

The Second World War did not end for everyone when the Japanese surrender was signed on the deck of the battleship *Missouri* on September 2, 1945. As we have seen in such films as *The Best Years of Our Lives,* the war continued to create problems for some time after it ended. The problems of reconversion from a wartime to peacetime footing were universal; the end of a war can have as dire consequences for the victor as for the vanquished, and Hollywood, as did the whole of America, faced a major readjustment both in priorities and product.

Films produced during the war were made with one goal in mind beyond profit—winning the fight. Propaganda had been the leading order of the day during most of the war years and it was only during the last six months and after the war that films were made which dealt with the war in realistic and serious terms. Only after the battles did anyone dare raise the larger questions about war and diplomacy. When we were fighting for survival no one would have listened,

Lana Turner and Clark Gable brought together by war duty in *Homecoming*.

everyone was too busy winning. But afterward, films like *The Searching Wind* asked questions; films like *The Best Years of Our Lives* confronted postwar human problems with candor, even in the context of entertainment; and films like *A Walk in the Sun* dealt with combat in tense realities.

This situation was not peculiar to World War II. The earlier "war to end all wars" had spawned three immensely popular films: *The Big Parade* (1925), *What Price Glory?* (1926) and *All Quiet on the Western Front* (1930). These films, which were also held in high critical regard, were made years after the war, during the peaceful time before the rise of the German Third Reich and the ominous turn of international events that presaged the second war. All three films dealt with war in realistic terms, stripping it of its glamour. *All Quiet on the Western Front* had reflected the pacifism of the American people, their disillusionment after World War I and the general feeling of the futility of war.

As with the first war, it was years after the fact that American films could look at the war with unblinking frankness and explore war and its effects in films like *Battleground* (1949) and *The Men* (1950), wherein Marlon Brando made his screen debut in Fred Zinneman's very excellent examination of paraplegic war veterans and the readjustment problems they faced.

When the full story of the Nazi liquidation of Europe's Jewish population became known with the liberation of the death camps, Hollywood responded with such films as *Crossfire* and *Gentlemen's Agreement,* which dealt with the problems and injustices caused by anti-Semitism. 1948's *Homecoming,* with Clark Gable and Lana Turner dealt with another wartime problem that was too touchy during the war itself as it explored personal relationships and marital infidelity resulting from husbands and wives being separated for long periods of time.

The film industry itself had some readjustment problems after the war. During the war years, despite the problems of wartime film production, despite restrictions and rationing, Hollywood prospered as never before. In 1946, the industry was riding the crest of a wave of wartime prosperity and its income reached record highs, stocks rose, and intoxicated from the huge profits of the war years, Hollywood ignored the distant early warnings about the potential impact of television on box-office revenues.

At the same time, foreign-made films began to achieve some popularity in the United States, providing unexpected competition for box-office dollars. The foreign film invasion began in earnest with the American success of *Open City* (1946), Roberto Rosselini's powerful story, parts of which were filmed before the war's end, of Italian resistance to the Nazis during the days just before the liberation by American and Allied forces.

After the war a general inflation set in and costs began to rise, wartime wage freezes were lifted and unions began to make up for lost time and wages in their postwar bargaining with the studios.

Hollywood was beset too with political problems. The House Committee on Un-American Activities began to investigate communism in the movie industry when cold war winds began to blow. Some of the people who a few years earlier had turned out films for the American war effort now found their patriotism called into question. Films such as *Mission to Moscow* and *The North Star* were seen through particularly jaundiced Congressional eyes; their makers were questioned about their political leanings and the intention behind their films. Dore Schary looks back at them with a little more logic than the Congressional inquisitors: "It was so stupid to think they were Russian propaganda; it would be like saying *Mrs. Miniver* was a plot to get us to become a monarchy. It's just crazy. These pictures were made to inspire audiences and make them aware of what was being done and the sacrifices that were being made by everybody, by the Russians and the Americans."

Congressional investigators and politicians took dimmer views of the purposes behind such films. Many industry personnel were called to testify. Some people pointed out suspected Communists in the ranks of Hollywood and admitted that, yes, they had, themselves, been concerned about the type of material that seemed to be emanating from some sources. These people who cooperated fully, and even enthusiastically, with the HUAC investigators became known as the "friendly witnesses." Among the "friendly witnesses" were Jack L. Warner (whose company had produced *Mission to Moscow*), directors Sam Wood (*For Whom the Bell Tolls*) and Leo McCarey, actors Adolph Menjou, Robert Taylor (who now regretted *Song of Russia*), Gary Cooper and Ronald Reagan.

Nineteen industry employees were suspected of "radical leanings" and considered "unfriendly witnesses" (In light of the accusations hurled at them, one hardly is surprised that they were "unfriendly" toward their accusers). Ultimately nine of the nineteen talked to the committee, but ten refused to testify. They maintained that the United States' Constitution made such questioning illegal itself. The ten remained "unfriendly" and went to jail on charges of contempt of Congress. These were Alvah Bessie, Herbert Biberman, Lester Cole, Edward Dmytryk, Ring Lardner, Jr., John Howard Lawson, Albert Maltz, Samuel Ornitz, Adrian Scott and Dalton Trumbo.

To protest the jailing of these people a Committee for the First Amendment was formed by about 500 industry personnel, but they too soon found themselves being called in for questioning. Some of them cooperated with the interrogators and added more names to the suspect lists. Among these cooperatives were Elia Kazan, Lee J. Cobb, Budd Schulberg, Sterling Hayden and Clifford Odets.

In Hollywood the "unfriendly" ten were blacklisted and for many years were not hired by the studios. (There were exceptions to the blacklisting, and from time to time it was rumored that a writer would be hired on the sly to beef up a script. One of the ten, director Dmytryk, changed his mind about remaining silent after serving part of his jail sentence and agreed to testify, whereupon he was dropped from the blacklist.) To prove its patriotism, Hollywood produced a few anti-communist pictures, mostly in the cloak-and-dagger espionage league, and a few ideological dramas of the nature of *My Son John* (1952) with Helen Hayes and Robert Walker. But as the home-front threat of communism diminished somewhat as an American political fetish and the fear of communist take-over abated, Hollywood turned to the real financial threat posed by the emergence of television, which brought with it a stunning decline in movie attendance and plunged the industry into both mental and economic depression and difficulties which have continued into the 1970s.

Looking back, one is impressed with the sense of community the war seemed to foster, not just in Hollywood but all over America. The United States presented a united front in facing its enemies who were very real and very tangible and very determined to conquer. The enemies were clearly perceived and the battle lines clearly drawn; they were the bad guys, we were the good guys, it was "cowboys and indians" and there was no question about it. In those unsophisticated times we were too busy fighting purely for self-survival to question the fight on less important intellectual terms. There were no anti-war films produced during World War II, because it was a very necessary and vital fight and after Pearl Harbor no American questioned our role. In the 1970s the enemies are less well-defined and indeed seem to be of our own creation when it comes to matters like over-population and environmental pollution and similar adversaries.

In 1973 the United States is extricating itself from a long, unpleasant, unpopular and, many claim, unnecessary military misadventure in Southeast Asia which has spawned no war film worth mentioning. Not even an anti-war film. Another time of disillusionment with war has set in as when *All Quiet on the Western Front* was made. And Dore Schary, who was there in Hollywood during those hectic, frantic and exciting war years, perhaps puts it all into perspective:

"You know you can make twenty of those [war, anti-war] pictures and you feel like Simon Bolivar on his deathbed; rejected, neglected, he referred to the series of revolutions that he had really created and said 'We have plowed the sea.' It's a marvelous metaphor; you go out and plow and plow and think you're making something and you look behind you and there's just plain water . . . nothing; you haven't done a goddamn thing. And it was René Clair, who said 'Nobody yet has made a good anti-war picture because we still have wars'."

The motion picture to end all wars obviously hasn't been made. But in Hollywood from roughly 1939 to 1945, many movies were made to win a war and until that ultimate anti-war film comes along, we're thankful for those that got us through.

The Pin Up Girls

Dorothy Lamour

Ann Sheridan

Jane Russell

Lana Turner

Veronica Lake

Hedy Lamarr

Rita Hayworth

Betty Grable

Ginger Rogers

Paulette Goddard